SCHLEIERMACHER

ABINGDON PILLARS
OF THEOLOGY

Schleiermacher

Terrence N. Tice

Abingdon Press
Nashville

SCHLEIERMACHER

This book is printed on acid-free paper.

Library of Congress Cataloging-in-Publication Data

Tice, Terrence N.
  Schleiermacher / Terrence N. Tice
    p. cm.—(Abingdon pillars of theology)
  Includes bibliographical references (p.   ) and indexes.
  ISBN 0-687-34334-8 (binding: paper: alk. paper)
  1. Schleiermacher, Friedrich, 1768–1834. I. Title. II. Series.

  BX4827.S3T53   2005
  230'.044'092—dc22

                                                                    2005019942

06 07 08 09 10 11 12 13 14 15—10 9 8 7 6 5 4 3 2 1
MANUFACTURED IN THE UNITED STATES OF AMERICA

In memory of

Mildred Dice Bennett,

my "book lady" as a youth

James I. McCord,

supportive colleague at Princeton and Geneva

CONTENTS

ABBREVIATIONS

BO   Friedrich Schleiermacher, *Brief Outline of Theology as a Field of Study* (1811, 1830). Translated by Terrence N. Tice. Lewiston, N.Y.: Edwin Mellen Press, 1990.

Br.   Edited by Ludwig Jonas and Wilhelm Dilthey. *Aus Schleiermacher's Leben in Briefen*. 2nd ed., 4 vols. Berlin: Reimer, 1860–1863. viii, 407; 513; x, 437; xvi, 646 S. [1st ed., vols. 1-2, 1858.]

CF   Friedrich Schleiermacher, *Christian Faith* (1821–1822, 1830–1831). Translated by Terrence N. Tice, Catherine L. Kelsey, and Edwina Lawler. Louisville: Westminster John Knox Press, 2005.

Ethics   Friedrich Schleiermacher, *Brouillon zur Ethik: Notes on Ethics* (1804–1806). Translated by John Wallhausser and Terrence N. Tice. Lewiston, N.Y.: Edwin Mellen Press, 2003. xiii, 289.

KGA   Schleiermacher, *Kritische Gesamtausgabe*.

OR   Friedrich Schleiermacher, *On Religion: Addresses in Response to its Cultured Critics*. 1821 edition. Translated by Terrence N. Tice. Richmond: John Knox Press, 1969. 363.

P.S.   Postscript (sections at the end of some propositions in *Christian Faith*).

Soliloquies   Friedrich Schleiermacher, *Soliloquies: An English Translation of the Monologen*. Translated by Horace Leland Friess. Chicago: Open Court, 1926. lx, 176.

SW   Schleiermacher, *Sämmtliche Werke*.

Chronology

Union of Reformed and Lutheran congregations at Dreifaltigkeitskirche	March 31, 1821
Trinity essay	1822
Christian Ethics lectures (Jonas ed.)	1822–1823
Christian Ethics lectures (Peiter ed.)	1826
Christmas Eve (2nd rev. ed.)	1827
"On the Glaubenslehre" essay	1829
Trip to England	1829
Speech at son Nathanael's grave	Nov. 1, 1829
Brief Outline (2nd rev. ed.), *Berliner Gesangbuch*	1830
Christian Faith, 2nd rev. ed.	1830–1831
Trip to Scandinavia	1833
Death	Feb. 12, 1834

INTRODUCTION

Friedrich Schleiermacher (1768–1834) is widely reputed to be the father of modern theology, somewhat on the analogy of the early church fathers. This little volume aims to show why. In an implicit dialogue with you, dear readers, it also hopes to enable you to decide in what ways he is also very much our contemporary, as a number of scholars believe he is today.

Since I was startled awake in discovering Schleiermacher exactly fifty years ago, I have sought chiefly to let him speak for himself. Early on, however, he lovingly reminded me that even such an effort must involve some interpretation. Dwelling within the consummatory stage of my own life, already a decade longer than his own life span of sixty-five, I still possess the considered desire to let him speak but this time in an interpretive mood that brings much that I have learned elsewhere to this very task. Thus, this summative work seeks not only to place this epoch-making thinker within his own context but also strives, at the same time, to interpret one who has by now become an old friend with an eye to our own context.

Although I cannot help drawing from my own numerous translations and writings centered on Schleiermacher's life and thought, these pages actually comprise a new work. Here I want freely and systematically to capture the nature, spirit, and impact of Schleiermacher's open-ended "system." As you will see, that system is anything but hidebound. Rather, even in its stringently historical-critical, scientific endeavors it intends to be warmly inclusive and, as we would say in these conflict-ridden days, ecumenical.

Before I first heard of Schleiermacher in 1955, I had already been powerfully influenced in my thinking by a seeming host of others, including the likes of all the major existentialists from Søren Kierkegaard to Gabriel Marcel, John Dewey (whose *Reconstruction of Philosophy* I read both ranting and exulting in the streets of Tucson), Friedrich Nietzsche (whose *Thus Spoke Zarathustra* took me on a sophomoric flight of self-discovery on desert stretches beyond the city), Martin Buber (himself greatly influenced by Schleiermacher, I later learned), Alfred North Whitehead, and R. G. Collingwood (my senior honors saint). At seminary my Princeton neoorthodox teachers engaged me, as did several kinds of philosopher, also New York's Reinhold Niebuhr and Paul Tillich, among others whose words and works I was devouring in a search to understand the Christian faith of my youth and the world of nuclear arms race and puzzling conflictual claims of "progress" all around me. Hundreds more have had an effect on me since that seminal moment, that positive shock of self-recognition, when I first read Schleiermacher's *Christian Faith* over several days (twice, scarcely stopping) under a great oak tree near Brown Hall. Then came doctoral study, above all the search of a barely confident "liberal" to find his way among more "conservative" leaders in the church and two years in Basel with Karl Barth, Karl Jaspers, and still other teachers. I prepared what turned out to be a rather wide-ranging dissertation inquiry on "Schleiermacher's Theological Method," and that truly launched me. I was then almost thirty years of age. The rest, as they say, is history.

Schleiermacher's Questions—and Ours?

By 1808, when Schleiermacher began his twenty-five-year career as theologian, philosopher, and historical scholar of ancient thought at the budding University of Berlin, he had reached the age of thirty-nine. As I will suggest here, conditions for the birth of modern theology can be seen in his life and thought more than a decade before that point. Thus, for two decades already, his mind and heart had been struggling with four main questions:

1. What has God done for us (Christians, human beings) in Christ?

2. How, then, should I be responding to this gift in my own life?

3. How am I to think out these two questions and the innumerable others that come to mind in this present age?

4. How might such thinking be related to our faith and life in the church and elsewhere?

How the Book Moves

The reflective answers to these questions and his methods for pursuing them that Schleiermacher passed on to us—perhaps in ways fitting to our own situations—is the main subject of this book. Although it moves in four parts that build on each other successively, these are also designed to be read in any order, according to interest. Occasionally I will stop to ask you to consider certain important issues.

1. It is necessary first to get an overview of Schleiermacher's early development, *as he saw it,* and his situation, activities, and scholarly efforts.

2. Famously, Schleiermacher roots his accounts of Christian faith and life in an "immediate existential relationship" with God, experienced distinctively by each individual within a distinct religious community. This experience he places in "immediate Christian religious self-consciousness." Thus, the next move must be to explain what Schleiermacher takes religious experience to be, more generally and in the collective life of Christians. Such a move is all the more called for in that this aspect of his theology is arguably the most important, yet it seems often to be the most egregiously misunderstood.

3. Then I present Schleiermacher's theology, as you might discover it in your own reading of his works, in a fairly tight successive unfolding of topics viewed from within his own ordering of priorities. To achieve this effect, I have found it necessary to reveal the logic he followed, as it were, in trying to understand Christian faith and life, though not strictly to replay the logic he chose in organizing *Christian Faith,* his chief theological work. In due course, then, something of what he explored in all the other parts of theology—all closely interconnected—is also folded in, especially from the inseparable companion lectures on Christian ethics, which he had only begun to put into published form before he died.

4. Finally, I have chosen to define several dozen major concepts present throughout Schleiermacher's very open "system," mostly, but not exclusively, inside theology. Although Schleiermacher's thinking moved over an astonishing range, it is all of one piece. Therefore, I am presenting these concepts in such a way that they can be read with profit in one fell swoop, from A to Z. Occasionally you may wish to skip around,

so I have tried to serve such moments of restless curiosity by indicating related items with an asterisk (*). These items can be found among the Definitions in chapter 4. In addition, throughout the text I have interspersed questions for reflection to help you process and think through Schleiermacher's concepts.

You are invited to make use of the bibliographical material and indexes so as to put together further pieces and to engage in further reflections for yourselves. Enjoy!

CHAPTER ONE

SCHLEIERMACHER'S LIFE AND CONTEXT

No choicer gift can any [person] give to another than [one's] spirit's intimate converse with itself. . . . In beholding [oneself a person] triumphs over discouragement and weakness, for from the consciousness of inner freedom there blossoms eternal youth and joy. On these have I laid hold, nor shall I ever give them up, and so I can see with a smile my eyes growing dim, and my blond locks turning white. Nought can happen to affright my heart, and the pulse of my inner life will beat with vigor until death. —Soliloquies, 9, 102-3

The Birth of Modern Theology in Schleiermacher's Person (1768–1796)

Childhood at Breslau and Pless (1768–1783)

Between the ages of eleven and twenty-eight (1780–1796) Friedrich Schleiermacher lived in ten municipalities, all quite different in size and quality of life. During that brief period we can witness the birth of modern theology in his person. I want to tell you highlights of this fascinating story and then, with equal brevity, tell you what happened afterward to consolidate the event. Given his background, Schleiermacher's options were always those of pulpit or podium alone. By 1808, when he was finally established at age thirty-nine in the city of Berlin, this once young genius was a well-known preacher and scholar. He was newly occupying both a pulpit at the Dreifaltigkeitskirche (Church of the Triune God) and a teaching position at the incipient University of Berlin, of which he was, in effect, the cofounder with Wilhelm von Humboldt, after whom the university is named today.[1]

Friedrich (Fritz) Schleiermacher was the eldest son of an eldest son, and third in a line of Reformed preachers. The restless independence of both his paternal forebears furnished little precedence toward settled orthodoxy; but three generations of calm, collected, deep-thinking Reformed pastors on the mother's side (Katharina-Maria Stubenrauch) proved a balance. An active Freemason and a moralistically oriented freethinker, his father, Gottlieb Schleiermacher, was a Reformed army chaplain in the large city of Breslau, where the family lived during most of Fritz's childhood, and was therefore often absent.

Little is known of Schleiermacher's childhood. We do know that his mother, who died on Nov. 17, 1783, was a very devout Christian and a superb caretaker of her three children: Charlotte (Lotte) (1765–1831), Friedrich (1768–1834), and Carl (1772–?). We also know that he bore a deep love for both parents. They, in turn, discovered Fritz's quick mind early and provided him a fine education, mostly at home, with tutoring, partly at boarding school.

The family first came into contact with the left-wing Reformation Herrnhuter Brethren church during the war of Bayer Succession in 1778, when they moved from Breslau to stay under protection of the Prince of Pless. Fritz was then nine years old. The Brethren colony of Gnadenfrei was nearby. In the spring of that year, Chaplain Schleiermacher experienced a deep-down conversion. This change to a firm and full belief in Christ as the Son of God and Reconciler of human beings to God turned the fifty-five-year-old pastor into a radical Herrnhuter, though he himself never joined the community. At Pless, in Fritz's eleventh year, many sleepless nights had brought him to a first inner transformation in his spiritual life, to a sense that eternal life comes not as a reward for virtue, as he had been taught, but by grace. He did not feel then, however, that he had received assurance of this grace, though he was profoundly convicted of sin. In 1780 Gottlieb prepared his daughter, Lotte, for confirmation using Herrnhuter material. He staunchly intended all his children to become Herrnhuters. Fritz, now fourteen, and Carl were brought by their parents to enter the small Brethren school and town of Niesky on July 14, 1783, there to receive instruction in the Christian faith. At Gnadenfrei, the school for girls, Lotte had preceded them on July 6. They were never to see their parents again.

Until April 5, 1783, when the family spent the two weeks before Easter at Gnadenfrei, their relation to the Brethren community (*Brüdergemeinde*) had been fairly indirect. Later, Schleiermacher was to regard this short stay as the birth of his "higher life." During a visit there in 1802 he wrote: "here my consciousness of the relation of human beings to a higher world first arose. . . . Here there first developed that mystical disposition which is so essential to me and has saved and preserved me under all the assaults of skepticism."[2] This was the second decisive change in his inner spiritual life. Only Lotte remained a Brethren throughout life. She and Fritz were in frequent contact. He visited her at Gnadenfrei five times between 1795 and 1811. From 1813 to 1825 she lived in his home and thereafter, until her death in 1831, at the Gemeindehaus in Berlin on Wilhelmstrasse. Carl made his own way and became a druggist.

Adolescence among the Brethren at Niesky and Barby (1783–1787)

Until the middle of his stay at Barby, Schleiermacher was an avid Herrnhuter, an experience that was hugely to mark his religious orientation the rest of his life. At the end he had totally broken with the narrow orthodoxy and biblical literalism he had also encountered there. By this period, there were some one hundred fifty German lands, which began to be consolidated only as Napoleon's armies swept across them two decades later. Dozens of mostly small, nonterritorial churches or sects existed among them, of which the Herrnhuter Brethren were notable for the high quality of their international work in education and missions and especially for their warm, enthusiastic, steadfast, and communal separatist piety. These Brethren had been expelled from Moravia by the Hapsburgs during the Thirty Years' War and had settled at Herrnhut, a small village built on the estates of Count Nikolaus Ludwig von Zinzendorf (1700–1760), who later became their bishop. A girls' school was founded at Gnadenfrei. Herrnhut and the work of this international community still exist today. Theirs has been a chiefly lyrical theology emphasizing communion with the "Savior," their heavenly Friend, discipleship, frequent singing and composing of songs, devotional exercise and hard, self-disciplined work. In Schleiermacher's day, belief in physical blood atonement was a strict test of membership. The staid orthodoxy he experienced in their company he later described as "the destructive principle in the community."[3] In contrast, he never gave up the experiential base of its communal piety. In his day worship was shared three or four times a day, up to seven times on festival days. At the stroke of midnight on New Year's, they all sang "Now Thank We All Our God" to the accompaniment of trombones, which also awakened them on Easter morning and welcomed them to the love feast and Lord's Supper. Weddings and funerals were also occasions for joyful celebration and for dressing in bright colors. In fact, joy was the central mood in all Herrnhuter worship, as in Schleiermacher's later popular work *Christmas Eve* (1806). He therefore came earnestly to accept these Brethren within the fold of the Evangelical church, just as they were.[4] In like fashion, after receiving nurture in Moravian Brethren piety with its assurance of grace, John Wesley had earlier had an experience of his heart being "strangely warmed." Not long after this experience on Aldersgate Street, Wesley visited Herrnhut, which further stimulated what he brought to the forming of Methodist practice. Wesley's relationship with Herrnhuter Brethren had occurred only fifty years before Schleiermacher's entry into Brethren schools.

At Niesky and Barby, Schleiermacher's devout sharing in communal piety represents his third major internal change. Moreover, within the school, where teachers were friends and pastors first and foremost, he developed further his own already strong self-discipline. As a consequence, there he "learned to contemplate the world from an idea out."[5] This meant not pure speculation but finding the originative or underlying or emerging principle of a person or process, such as the "idea" of Christianity—a fourth major turn. Like everyone, he studied a very wide array of subjects but was also free to pursue his own interests, which for him included Hebrew and English besides the required Greek, Latin, and French. On December 1, 1784, among the ninety-eight students were ten Danish, seven English, two Dutch, and three Swiss, and eleven were of missionary families from the Americas—this in a village of six hundred. A large percent of the students were of the aristocracy. The greatly revered overseer Theodor Christian Zembsch, who taught Schleiermacher Hebrew, Greek, and Latin, was like a second father to him. The young philosopher-historian, Karl G. Garve (1763–1841) was also important in his life. His special friend was Johann Baptist von Albertini (1769–1830), later bishop of the *Brüdergemeinde* and the most famous writer of religious songs in his time. From January 1784 they read the first half of the Old Testament together, then from August 1784, for a year, Greek literature, in both cases using only a grammar and a lexicon. The latter project began his lifelong studies in Greek. The former project led to an unbroken considerable appreciation of the Hebrew Bible for understanding the background of Christianity. However, in 1829 he also stated: "This conviction that in its advance vital Christianity needs no support whatsoever taken from Judaism is as old with me as my religious consciousness itself."[6]

When, after two years, the two friends were promoted to the school primarily aimed at educating Brethren schoolmasters and pastors, within a *Gemeinde* of two hundred souls lodged near the secular city of Barby, the situation was quite similar except that students were restricted as to where they could wander and what they could read. Classmates Beyer, Zaezlin, the Englishman Samuel Okely, Schleiermacher, and Albertini formed a clandestine philosophical club. There they could read forbidden books by current authors such as Goethe and Wieland and could discuss what they pleased. Eventually, Okely, a brilliant devotee of Jean-Jacques Rousseau, openly protested against some "false beliefs" of the community and was thereupon sent home on Dec. 3, 1786, where he died in a drowning accident in the summer of 1787. This event deeply affected Schleiermacher, who was from September 1786 also struggling mightily over orthodox beliefs within himself and in discussion with his teachers and comrades, then through correspondence with his father.[7] During December and January he less dramatically announced his own negation of "supernatural feelings,"[8] the classical two natures doctrine of Christ's divinity, total corruption and eternal punishment—all Brethren fundamentals—together with his conviction that "in good conscience" he could no longer remain at Barby. He was never to return to these beliefs, though he considered his faith and his attendant grasp of the inner meaning of Christianity to be sound. This "first flowering of the spirit" led to a "crucial act" described in the *Soliloquies*:

> While enjoying the beautiful freedom of youth I succeeded in the crucial act of casting off the mummery in which long and tedious hours of educational sacrilege had clothed me; I learned to deplore the brief independence enjoyed by the majority of [persons] who allow themselves to be bound by new chains; I learned to despise the contemptible efforts of the lifeless, who have forgotten even the last trace of the brief dream of freedom, who mistake what transpires in youth when freedom is just awakening and wish to keep the young faithful to old ways.[9]

The club was in effect soon disbanded. Beyer went to Jena. Schleiermacher left in April, after a period from late January on in which he was forbidden to participate in *Gemeine* activities or to discuss his doubts with comrades until he relented. He did not. On January 17 he carefully, tenderly informed his father of his radical turn of faith, the fifth major transformation in his spiritual life. His father reacted in a violent repudiation of his son, which he did not rescind until shortly before his death on Sept. 2, 1794. Despite his explanation that he could not believe in doctrines that lacked support "on critical, exegetical and philosophical grounds," and must break with that "alien yoke" of the past,[10] his father could only retort that he had become "a denier of God."[11] Schleiermacher was then eighteen. The painful break had been accomplished, but unceasingly over the rest of his life he was to remain "a Herrnhuter, only of a higher order."[12]

The Young Scholar at Halle and Drossen
(April 1787–April 1790)

Schleiermacher's father did agree to his desire to attend the University of Halle, a few miles distant, where he lived in the warm, cordial home of his uncle Samuel Ernst Timotheus Stubenrauch (1738–1807), a professor of church history there. He had a small garret room to himself, there to prepare for theological examinations and for tutoring in some noble house. Halle was a sufficiently sizeable town to have a large military installation. The heyday of pietism had long since passed there, though it had laid the groundwork for all subsequent developments at the University, including those of the leading German Enlightenment figures Gottfried Wilhelm Leibniz (1648–1716) and his chief purveyor Christian Wolff (1679–1754). Many of its professors were experiential, practical-minded men, as Schleiermacher would become from this time on, a sixth inner transformation of his life easily combined with a strong theoretical interest. In his chosen concentration on classical studies and philosophy he was able to garner much to think with from the noted practitioner of philological criticism Friedrich August Wolf (1759–1824)[13] and even more from Johann August Eberhard (1739–1809), then the most noted member of the faculty and a Wolffian philosopher who also published theological works. Schleiermacher took everything Eberhard had to offer—ethics, history of philosophy, epistemology (called *Aesthetik*), and even a course on synonyms. At its peak enrollment of 1,156 in 1786, 800 were theological students, including auditors from philosophy and classical philology, but Schleiermacher engaged in very little theological coursework. He did, however, work more on his English and French in anticipation of a tutoring position.

In the Autumn of 1788 his uncle took a pastorate in Drossen. Schleiermacher was left to his own devices until May 1789, when he traveled the long distance northeast to Drossen, walking the last four miles from Frankfurt-an-Oder. In Drossen he was to live the next year in a small, cozy room lined with his uncle's books, preparing for two successive examinations in theology. The most important event during the otherwise rather melancholy time in Halle on his own was a very typical one throughout life: he formed a close and permanent friendship. Okely had drowned. Contact with Albertini was spotty, and they did not see each other again until 1822. So, the continual, abiding relationship with Carl Gustav von Brinckmann (1764–1841), a Swedish diplomat, is a signal event, worthy of being termed a seventh major turning point in his inner life. His new friend, also an ex-Herrnhuter, introduced him to cultured circles in Halle and introduced him to the fascinating new world of women. In return, Schleiermacher brought to him his burgeoning thought and a deepened "sense for the holy."

Even in Drossen, however, theology received only intermittent attention. He received greater satisfaction from reading ancient writers and Immanuel Kant (1724–1804), whose three great *Critiques* on pure and practical reason and on judgment had appeared in 1781, 1785, and 1788. Kant was both an inspiration and a foil for much that he was thinking about. At least five draft essays flew from his pen. The gratification from such generativity I regard to be an eighth major event in his inner spiritual life, though the mode of expression on such subjects as human nature, freedom, morality, justice, and the highest good was philosophical. As for theology, he was getting his "critical," non-Enlightenment, nonrationalist, nonsupernaturalist, nonbiblicist bearings there too. He was crossing the Rubicon from pure philosophy to the experience of faith and then, standing on faith but with eyes wide open to both sides of the river, was beginning to work out a theological position not strictly reducible to *any* traditional frame of reference from Origen to Aquinas to Calvin and Luther to the Protestant scholastics to more recent theologians. He had a long way to go before he could articulate all this, but there is clear evidence, for example, in a letter to

Brinckmann of September 28, 1789, that he had struck a path that he could regard as relevant to his own time. Because this was not a merely philosophical or intellectual move but a distinct expression of faith, I think of this move as a ninth major development in his spiritual life. These two moves, which derive from his experiences and reflections at Halle and Drossen, I have called his "critical realism."

A tenth inner development also began in Drossen: his first extended close relationship with a woman. In Halle he learned that he could converse on important subjects with cultured folk and, through his friend's confidences and introductions, especially with women. At Drossen, in the summer of 1789, he found among his uncle's relatives in nearby Landsberg an der Warthe the beautiful, mature, intelligent wife of a civil servant, Frau Beneke. Much in this woman's home, at first busying himself with attempts to tutor her small daughter, he was very much taken with her and she, unhappy in marriage at that time and having unfulfilled needs, was on the brink of divorce and was more than drawn to him. In already characteristic fashion, he talked the whole matter out with her, and she wonderingly listened to his sober, patient advice. Frau Beneke was later to thank him for saving her marriage. During his future stay in Landsberg, as assistant to her father, uncle Stubenrauch's brother-in-law, Pastor Schumann (1794–1796), he was more often in the Beneke house, an endeared friend of the whole family. The two regularly corresponded until 1801.[14] Other such relationships, as in her case not all fully romantic, were to follow in fairly quick succession. "Only through knowledge of the inner spirit of women," he wrote in 1802, "have I gained knowledge of the true worth of a human being."[15] In 1799, he wrote: "It lies very deep in my nature that I should always attach myself more closely to women than to men, for there is so much in my spirit that men rarely understand."[16]

On to Berlin (1790): A Six-Month Interlude

In April Schleiermacher went to Berlin, where he passed his first theology exams in May and preached his examination sermon on July 15. Brinckmann was also in Berlin that summer and no doubt introduced him to some of the cultured leaders of this bustling, worldly city of 100,000, especially to Enlightenment figures whom he knew and whose work Schleiermacher had been reading. Now twenty-one, Schleiermacher wanted to stay there, but Bishop Friedrich Samuel Gottfried Sack (1738–1817) found him an excellent tutoring position at the faraway country estate of Count von Dohna at Schlobitten in East Prussia, so there he went.

Schlobitten (1790–1793) and Berlin Again (1793–1794)

At Schlobitten Schleiermacher found a pious, gracious, energetic high aristocratic family of ten, surrounded with beauty and living in simple luxury. He took on education of six children, lived intimately with the family, had a daily game of chess with the count, and preached every other Sunday. Leaving on good terms in the spring of 1793, he taught religion and mathematics (a subject he had always loved) at a Berlin Gymnasium in exchange for petty cash and membership in the famous Gedike seminar for teachers. Then he got a better job in the Kornmesser Orphanage, where he had lodging and time to prepare for the second round of theology exams, which he finished on March 31, 1794. The overall performance had advanced from "very good" the first time to "brilliant" in the end. In Landsberg Pastor Schumann needed an assistant, so this appointment was arranged and Schleiermacher returned there in April 1794.

At Schlobitten everything would have seemed routine, interesting, even glorious on the surface of his life. Underneath, tremendous, life-changing events were occurring. It is certainly noteworthy that during those three years he had the experience of helping children initially aged 9, 10, 14, 15, 16, and 20 years. He had the pleasure of conversation with intelligent, sharp-witted Caroline (20) and was inspired and smitten by Friederike, at 16 already marvelously gifted of spirit. (She died in 1801.) He also began a lifelong friendship with two older sons, Alexander and Wilhelm. All this experience would have been sufficient to stimulate his ultimately progressive and developmental sense of educational process, the theory of which he eventually became famous for in German educational circles. Here we focus on two inner transformations that were contributive to all his thought, including that in education.

So, the eleventh transformation in his inner spiritual life, which he took from his Schlobitten experience, was a deep sense for human community—first in a family and also between a man and a woman. In the *Soliloquies* he summarized this awakening:

> In a stranger's home my sense for the beauty of [communal existence] was first awakened; I saw that it requires freedom to ennoble and give right expression to the delicate intimacies of human nature, which remain forever obscure to the uninitiated who [often endure] them [as natural restrictions more than they respect them]. Amid all the [diversity] of this world's motley spectacle I learned to discount appearances and to recognize the same reality whatever its garb, and I also learned to translate the many tongues that it acquires in various circles.[17]

In an essay, "On What Gives Value to Life" (1792–1793), first written in this period, he had also stated, "You, quiet joys of shared activity and shared feeling, remain the crown of my life! . . . Whenever I reflect on all life's manifold gifts and quite conscientiously analyze what value each has, the finest gift ever remains that a person can be at home [*hauslich*]."[18] Both quotations indicate that his primary experiential source for the new insight was life with the eight von Dohna children, their forty-year-old mother and the older count.

The twelfth insight broadened out from this source, based on his occupations with the thought of Kant and Eberhard from his time at Halle and issuing in three finished essays he had intended to publish in a collection. These were first published in full only in 1984, in KGA I/1: "On the Highest Good" (1789), "On Freedom" (1790–1792), and then "On What Gives Value to Life." The twofold insight is that we are all members of one humanity and that freedom is not transcendental, not something to be postulated above and beyond our ordinary life, contrary to Kant, but is an essential aspect of our own real existence. Later he termed this discovery "species-consciousness*." We are all members of one large community, discovered and expressed locally. The distinctly new value theory he formed at the end of this series of experiences, moreover, places the focal values of human life not in pleasure or happiness, contrary to Aristotle and others, but in the pursuit of what is good, that is, important for human growth. Furthermore, human life at its best is shared. Thus, he introduces a lengthy statement on this in the *Soliloquies* with these words: "To behold humanity [in] oneself. . . . This vision is the intimate and necessary tie between conduct and the perception of truth. . . . A truly human way of acting produces a clear consciousness of [the humanity in me], and this in turn permits of no other behavior than such as is worthy of humanity."[19] Then he recalls the moment in which he gained this consciousness: "The sublime revelation came from within; it was not produced by any code of ethics or system of philosophy. My long quest, which neither this nor that would satisfy was crowned in one moment of insight; freedom dissolved my dark doubts in a single act." Yet he goes on in such a way as to indicate that his understanding was still unsettled, and we will shortly come to see why. The stumbling block was his belief in universally articulable reason, in the sense that we are simply all "of one substance," "inwardly altogether alike" even in all our incidental diversity.

Landsberg an der Warthe (1794–1796)

Although he was appointed to assist the ailing Pastor Schumann, almost as soon as he had returned to Landsberg an der Warthe in April 1794 Schleiermacher was doing everything, and he was very well received. In off hours he was reading up on the controversy then raging over Baruch Spinoza's cohesive deterministic view of God, human life, and the world. This view could lead to pantheism, but would it have to? Schleiermacher was, and remained, a monotheist. He believed that God had provided, and was providing, a world in which human freedom could thrive. Perhaps a modified Spinozistic determinism could account for his newly discovered sense for a general humanity, but could it leave room for freedom, and would affirming human freedom be enough? By itself, freedom could not "straightaway" enable one to rise "to the still higher level of individuality in growth and morality" or enable one to grasp that "higher existence," or "distinctive nature," which freedom might choose for itself in each individual. So, ironic as it may seem, very likely it was precisely his occupation with determinism that led him to his "highest intuition," which never left him. As he puts it in the *Soliloquies* passage to which I have just been referring:

> The sense of freedom alone did not content me. . . .
> Thus there dawned upon me what is now my highest intuition [*höchste Anschauung**]. I saw clearly that *each [person] is meant to represent humanity in [one's] own way*, combining its elements uniquely, so that it may reveal itself in every mode, and all that can issue from its womb [will] be made actual in the fullness of [infinity] [1822: the infinity of space and time]. This thought alone [1822: above all] has uplifted me, and set me apart from everything common and untransformed in my surroundings; it has made of me a . . . creation of the [deity] [1810, 1822: through it I feel myself to be an elect creation of the deity], rejoicing in a [distinctive] form and [development] *[Bildung]*. The act of freedom [that] accompanied this [perception] has assembled . . . the elements of human nature [about it and inwardly conjoined them] to [form] a [distinctive] existence.[20]

Both a philosopher and a theologian are talking here. As a philosopher doing "ethics" writ large (that is, the human sciences), Schleiermacher is affirming that a deterministic view of human behavior can be made compatible with human freedom. This does not mean that all human behavior is predictable. It does mean that the system of reality in which human behavior takes place is inescapably interconnected. As a theologian he is adding, as he later puts the matter in *Christian Faith* (1821 §9; 1830 §4): we feel ourselves to be "absolutely dependent" but only "relatively," never absolutely, "free." Thereby, from a Christian point of view, each of us is seen to exist "in relation to God" and thus to be "an elect creation" of God. This insight represents the thirteenth major shift in Schleiermacher's inner spiritual life during the period from age eleven to no more than twenty-seven. During the Landsberg period we see, notably in the 1795 and 1796 Ascension Sunday sermons, that the mainspring of a true Christian religious life and morality is Christ, the focal figure of his overall sermon production since the first record appears in 1789.

Now, by 1795 or 1796, we have reached the end of our quest. Although, for the most part, these thirteen transformations in Schleiermacher's inner spiritual life are not, and were not meant to be, expressed in theological terms, virtually everything is in place for what I am calling the birth of modern theology. All these elements of his faith experience were to be consolidated and expressed in future years as he moved into more outwardly and specifically theological work. Moreover, although the details of his vision of religion and church in *On Religion* (1799) probably did not come into clear focus until shortly before he began writing, the essential principles that obviously guided the main configuration there were already obvious to him at least three years earlier.

The Middle Years (1796–1807)

Berlin and Stolpe (1796–1804)

Heretofore the progression of Schleiermacher's insights and inner life closely followed upon his successive moves to new settings. This process continued in subsequent years, yet not so as greatly to modify the inner consciousness and faith he had discovered by 1796. Moreover, already in the initial autumn months of his unusually extended stay in Berlin (1796–1802) the now twenty-seven-year-old pastor was openly employing the juxtaposition of inner and outer elements to which I have referred. In all the years to follow it was to burgeon forth in a thousand forms, spreading its tendrils over nearly every area of his philosophical and theological work and forming the foundation for his constant, tireless observation of others and of himself. From here on, therefore, I can restrict myself to a brief account of mostly external events and factors. A more extensive treatment would, of course, reveal the interaction of both internal and external ingredients of his ongoing life. His was not the first great mind to reach its basic, lifelong disposition by his twenties; for example, Descartes did so and presumably Plato. Some, like Freud and Barth, came to this point a bit later. Others never reach such a solid achievement of personal identity. When Schleiermacher, at twenty-seven, took up his second very busy six-year pastorate, at Charity Hospital in Berlin, he immediately began a lively engagement with the city's cultured life, the "free sociality" of its salons, contributing especially to the signally creative activity of the early German Romantic movement (which also thrived mostly from 1796 to 1802 there). He came into all this markedly mature in his faith and philosophy, with readiness for intense, deep-going friendship, and openness to a wide diversity of views and lifestyles. In particular, he was in no mood to have "romanticism" mold him; instead, insofar as he could, he helped mold romanticism, especially as a critical realist and as a profoundly moral and religious thinker, not as one primarily oriented to letters and the arts.

Thus, he embarked enthusiastically into a breathtaking series of studies, reviews, and "fragments" (according to a style frequently used in the Romantic's periodical *Athenaeum*, 1798–1800). At the behest of Bishop Sack, he translated several volumes of sermons by the famous pulpit orators Hugo Blair and Joseph Fawcett, from Edinburgh and Halifax. With his incipient lifelong friend Henriette Herz he also translated some English travel books about Africa and North America. In 1799 and 1800 he published essays arguing on behalf of full civil rights for Jews and for women. Ah yes, and he also fell in love, this time with a woman grievously trapped in an arranged marriage to another pastor. Her name was Eleonore von Grunow. Schleiermacher agonizingly waited for six years for her to make up her mind to marry him. At just the point when he had reason to be most hopeful she finally backed off. This great loss, like the earlier losses of his mother in 1783 and his father in 1794, became a spur to creative activity unusual even for him, and the most immediate result was his last of several rhapsodic works, *Christmas Eve* (1806), and his decision to stop trying to write poetry and to devote himself to biblical preaching, to ecclesial and civic affairs, and to the "scientific" work of theology and philosophy instead. His greatest works of the middle period in Berlin were in his rhapsodic, yet carefully thought-out popular volumes: *On Religion* (written in two month's time, February to April 1799, and published later that year) and the *Soliloquies* (completed in less than one month in the fall of 1799, published as "A New Year's Gift" in 1800), each of which became so famous that he offered each in two further, revised editions. Together those two books comprised a manifesto for his subsequent career. Meanwhile, over these six years in Berlin he continued to accrue invaluable experience on a daily basis, visiting and praying chiefly with the poor and with others sick of body or mind in a general hospital (the Charité Krankenhaus), preaching and conducting the full round of pastoral care.

During all the years Schleiermacher lived in Berlin the city too was growing, in both size and stature. In this first period, the king was having great monumental structures built as the city expanded in stature, still surrounded by a wall but entered from the west through the Brandenburg Gate. Most of these structures are still standing in the city center today, in service of the university, government, churches, and the arts. The hospital was a short walk from them all.

Stolpe (1802–1804): An Isolated Interlude

In 1802, partly to get Schleiermacher away from Eleonore von Grunow, Bishop Sack sent him to a very small parish in Stolpe, on the far distant northern coast of Prussia. This was the only assignment he ever had in which there was very little to do. So, exiled as it were, he turned to his studies. In 1803 he published a 350-page volume offering *Foundations for a Critique of Previous Ethical Theory*, which chiefly presents logical and other difficulties inherent in these theories without revealing his own. He also began what proved to be the classic translation of Plato into German, which is still widely used (1804–1809, 1828), and pursued other inquiries. In 1804 he issued a 200-page examination regarding the background of Protestant church-state relations and prospects for church union.

Preacher and Professor at the University of Halle (1804–1806)

In response, in part, to political developments in France, the Prussian king determined to engage in moral reforms in Prussia. As part of this effort he encouraged more worship and decreed that the University at Halle would begin holding services led by a University preacher. In 1804 Schleiermacher was appointed to be the first University preacher at Halle, the only Reformed pastor in the midst of a faculty of Lutheran theologians. They resisted his offering services but could not prevent him from offering lectures. It took two years before worship was held in the University, beginning August 3, 1806. By mid-September 1806 the chapel was needed to store grain for the Prussian army. Thus, services were held off-campus until Napoleon's army marched into Halle on October 17 and closed the University entirely. Although Schleiermacher's freer pedagogy was strikingly opposite to the methods of his conservative colleagues, students stayed away from his lectures on dogmatics or theological encyclopedia the first two terms. Halle was a Lutheran University, and suspicious Lutherans were calling him such things as an atheist, a Spinozist, a Herrnhuter, a Reformed heretic, and a crypto-catholic. Ethics, given during the first two winter semesters, had fared better, attracting fifty students the second time. In summer semester, 1805, he had also offered a course in hermeneutics, as a first step in his plan to offer a constructive, nonphilological, one-year course on the whole New Testament, which he was never able to carry out. His public exegesis course on Galatians that fall was the most popular, drawing 120 members. At Halle, his instruction was to center on New Testament studies, which he believed should be the fundament of a person's entire theological work. He would concentrate on exegesis, practical theology, and a critical handling of dogmatics, he thought. His function would be to help students learn for themselves. His first contribution was to be an extensive study of Paul's Letters. He hoped soon to understand Paul as well as he did Plato. He had begun this process in the summer term, 1806, in addition to courses on Christian ethics, dogmatics, and church history. Between semesters he had spent a great deal of time on Plato. Then on October 17, 1806, Napoleon's invasion of Halle intervened. Napoleon, eager to conscript young men in the town and not to face local opposition, ordered that the University be shut down.

That fall of 1806 saw the appearance of the *Christmas Eve* "dialogues," conceived in a flash after attending a concert by the famous blind flutist Dulon and written in a few days. Imagined on the heels of losing Eleonore, the dialogues were placed in a beautiful scene of domesticity, with friends wherein the theme was the meanings of Christmas. Stories were told by the women, accounts were given by the men. The scene was joyous and full of music, though there were rumblings of the French juggernaut. Now that the French had arrived, Schleiermacher changed his center of operation from podium to pulpit. The sharp, passionate ring of his patriotic sermons, preached to a group of educated people who had much idealism and world-citizenry in their blood but little patriotism and who were initially entranced by Napoleon's power, made him a national figure almost overnight.

By early 1807 there was no way to sustain himself in Halle, so he returned to Berlin. As things transpired, he was to remain there for the rest of his life. From now on, Schleiermacher was always writing something. *Christmas Eve* was the swan song of rhapsody and attempts at poetry, exchanged for science, preaching, pastoral work, and public affairs. Appearing in 1807 were his extraordinary critical works on *I Timothy* and on *Heraclitus*; issued in 1808 were the second collection of sermons and his book-length essay presenting *Occasional Thoughts on Universities*. His uncle Stubenrauch, to whom he had promised the volume of sermons, died in 1807.

Was his Romanticism dead then? By no means! It was only rechanneled. Like Novalis and other contemporary Romantic literary figures, like the painter Caspar David Friedrich, and especially like the great composer Ludwig van Beethoven, the mature Schleiermacher had become a virtually self-made Romantic, both in his self-expression in the *Soliloquies* and in his aesthetic awareness and theory. Yet, like Beethoven he also incorporated more classical themes within his reportoire. This comparison with Beethoven is no accident, for three reasons. First, he was steeped in what we would call "classical" music. During the Halle years he had been a frequent evening guest at Gebiechenstein, the house of the Reichardt family, there for evening performances. In Berlin he often attended concerts, and he sang tenor for many years in the Singakademie. Second, he took music to be an immediate expression of his religious sensibility. Third, like Beethoven, who was conversant with Schleiermacher's aesthetic views through his close friend Friedrich August Kanne, he had learned how to replace sheer reason with imagination, but, partly in contrast to Beethoven, he also learned how to keep them together. Therein lies the genius of his later years. Beethoven's biographer wrote of Beethoven:

> In his earlier years, a relatively unmediated adherence to reason and virtue acted as a powerful organizing principle of his creativity as well as an eventual constraint on its further development. In the course of time, as the so-called heroic style (ca. 1803–13) moved toward exhaustion, Beethoven found a collateral organizing principle in the idea of the imaginative, seen as an adjunct to reason, as an unfettered instrument of investigation with the power of representing a multitude of previously undescribed modes of being and strategies of transcendence.[21]

With slight emendation, this statement could also be made of Schleiermacher.

The Later Berlin Years (1808–1834)

During all of Schleiermacher's stays in Berlin the city was growing.[22] By 1800 the population had grown to 172,122, of which 25 percent were children and youth, 14 percent were military personnel and 8 percent required public assistance. In 1808–1809 ten thousand French soldiers were quartered there, the officers in middle-class households, most of the rest in barracks. There was a population increase of 65 percent between 1809 and 1816, to about 283,000. By 1834 it had more than doubled (from 1809) to more than 350,000. Through this latter period Berlin households held an average of twenty-one persons living in three-story buildings.

In Berlin, the pace of change in Schleiermacher's life quickened for a few years, but it never got to settle into an even flow, despite the unstinting regularity of his work habits. Fortunately, he could usually get by on four or five hours of sleep, so after the activities of the day, public and domestic, he could spend the wee hours of the night thinking and writing, then often rise to meet his classes between 6:00 and 9:00 in the morning. He greatly preferred the direct contact of teaching and preaching to writing.

In 1808 he was already teaching at the incipient University of Berlin, now possessing the only theology department in Prussia. By the king's order of May 28, 1808, issued as patron of the Dreifaltigkeitskirche (Church of the Triune God), a mixed Lutheran and Reformed church and one of the largest in Berlin, Schleiermacher was called to a pastorate of the Reformed congregation there, subject to its right of refusal. The previous pastor had died. Thus, according to the custom, he had to wait a year to enable assistance to the widow and to take up his position officially. He already began his work as pastor, however, in the fall of 1808. His official beginning occurred on June 11, 1809. As a consequence, despite such waiting, now he had both podium and pulpit going. In addition, even before he was made secretary of the University's founding committee, he was pouring heart and soul into that activity as well. He also got married.

The final twenty-five years of Schleiermacher's career may best be conveyed briefly in several categories, beginning with his family life.

Family

Schleiermacher remained unmarried until age forty. He met Henriette Sophie Elizabeth von Muehlenfels (1788–1840), the woman who was to be his wife, in 1804 during a beautiful summer's intermezzo on the isle of Rügen far south along the North Sea coast on his way from Stolpe to Halle. She, then sixteen, became the wife of his friend Ehrenfried von Willich. Thence began a warmly affectionate "father-daughter" correspondence that has become a classic in its own right. Von Willich died in 1807, leaving her with two very small children. In 1808 she accepted Schleiermacher's proposal of marriage. They were married on May 18, 1809.

In addition to Henriette's two children, Ehrenfried and Henriette von Willich, they had four further issue: Clara Elizabeth (1810–1881), married name Besser; Hanna Gertrud (1812–1839), married name Lommatzsch; Hildegard Marie (1817–1889), who became Gräfin Schwerin in 1834; and Nathanael Hermann (1820–1829). For long periods the household included Schleiermacher's half sister "Nanny" (Anne Maria Louise) Schleiermacher (1786–1869), later married name Arndt, or his sister Lotte (see above), and the somewhat problematic widow Karoline Fischer, born Lommatzsch, and her daughter Luise. Frau Fischer came as an elder companion to his wife, problematic in that she had a strong presence and tended to draw Henriette in directions, including religious ones, not favorable to him, but they worked out a way for her to stay. In 1817 they all moved to larger quarters within the household of his publisher, Georg Reimer, where they remained. A full description of Schleiermacher's principles for *The Christian Household* (1820) exists in a series of sermons from 1818. By all accounts, including those of his son Ehrenfried (1909), he kept to his principles. It was a warm, busy household, the marriage was loving and sound, and he was much engaged with this large family. For additional companionship, Schleiermacher enjoyed numerous friends and colleagues in his "outside, public" life. Frequently he had a friend or students "in" for lunch or tea. There were family trips, to Rügen and other distant places in German lands, concerts and various public events. He was, as before, often in the home of his closest female friend, the cultured hostess Henriette Herz.

From 1804 on, Schleiermacher's ethical (human sciences) accounts based all other large social institutions on family life. The others, to be noticed in order here, were the church, science and education, free sociality, and the state. Today his divisions would no doubt contain a great many more elements, even more complexly related, but they encompass his life in these years very well.

Church

Visitors and residents from other parts of the city came to hear Schleiermacher. My favorite image is of this Geneva-tabbed preacher in his high pulpit directly facing mostly servants at the third rank of seats, which were free. The other seats were rented. The sermons ran between roughly thirty and forty-five minutes. His actual parish extended from Hallisches Tor (gate) in the south, forming a triangle along the western city wall, through the city's busiest intersection at today's Potsdamer Platz north to the Behrenstrasse (one block south of the Brandenburg Gate and parallel to Unter den Linden), east on the Behrenstrasse to Friedrichstrasse and then straight south back to Hallisches Tor. The University was situated two blocks further east of the Friedrichstrasse on Unter den Linden, just outside his parish. Most of the government and cultural buildings were on either side of Unter den Linden. These monumental structures are still in place today. The round church building where Schleiermacher served was destroyed in World War II by stray bombs, which were intended for newer governmental buildings nearer the old western city wall. The cemetery, where his large gravestone remains, was just outside the wall several blocks away. The three-story parsonage, several blocks from the church at the corner of Taubenstrasse and the current Glinkastrasse, still stands, but some of its many windows have been walled over. In the years before Napoleon's final defeat in 1815, the city had a paucity of horses, taken for the war. In 1811 the king freed the Prussian peasants from serfdom to win them over to his side. In succeeding years they poured into Berlin in droves. The burden of taxes levied by the king to pay for the war and for reparations to Napoleon was carried by its citizens for several decades to come. From childhood through the rest of his life, Schleiermacher had ready evidence around him of the terrible violence and ravages of war. Church and state alone offered him conflict enough to fuel his deep desire for nonviolence at all levels of life and his active commitment to loving, civil modes of resolution consonant with his Christian faith.

As Andreas Reich (1992) has shown, Schleiermacher was constantly involved in most aspects of pastoral service and was active at all levels of church government. In some years he had an assistant; when not, he did it all. He conducted worship and preached nearly every Sunday, which yielded almost six hundred published sermons and outlines from 1787 to 1834 and more than one hundred fifty not yet dug out of archives (see Tice, 1997, for a detailed account). Within the church itself there were issues concerning care of widows, orphans, and the poor; major repairs of the building; organ restoration; pew rentals; disturbance of services by street noise; general decision-making; conduct of funerals and sacraments; and instruction for confirmation. Outside there were involvements in conflict over liturgical agenda proposed by the king and in other matters in which Schleiermacher strove to form an effective polity both to oppose imposition of various rules from authorities and, thereby, protect congregational autonomy in worship and local governance and also to obviate strife due to confessional differences. Because of these activities he suffered persecution that threatened loss of his academic and pastoral positions, even his citizenship.

He was a prominent leader in all these situations, was generally successful, and, accordingly, was generally held in great honor. The historian Leopold von Ranke estimated that at his death at least twenty thousand persons followed his casket through the streets of Berlin. The queen's carriage was particularly conspicuous within this astonishing entourage. Standing up to the king, earlier his strong advocate, led to occasional disfavor in relation to the state so that he had never received royal awards that a public servant of his eminence ordinarily enjoyed. He did receive a minor award in 1830. The Church of the Triune God, which he served as copastor, was the first to attain union between Lutheran and Reformed congregations in Prussia, a union celebrated on March 31, 1822. After union, his duties increased, for now they were less restricted to the smaller Reformed congregation. In 1830 he completed years of labor on a famed hymnal, the *Berliner Gesangbuch*. No doubt his most enduring legacy from all this effort, however, lies in his preaching.

The University, the Academy, and Education

In effect, Schleiermacher was cofounder, with Wilhelm von Humboldt, of the University of Berlin. In 1808, he published *Occasional Thoughts on Universities*, which quickly became the most influential set of principles and proposals for a truly liberal institution at that time, and he was named secretary of the organizing committee. He then served in other related capacities, to secure what had been at first somewhat tenuously established, long after von Humboldt had left after 16 months on this job. After the University's official opening in 1810 he was responsible for organizing the theology faculty, serving as its dean in 1810–1811, then 1813–1814, 1817–1818, and 1819–1820. He served as rector for the University as a whole in 1815–1816. In addition, he joined the short-lived Stein reform government in 1808. Known as a patriot since the Halle days, in Berlin he also served as a spy and secret correspondent during the Napoleonic era there. From 1808 on, through his writings and lectures he came to be known as the most eminent advocate of progressive education at all levels in German lands.

On almost all public issues, his colleague, the philosopher Georg Wilhelm Friedrich Hegel (1770–1831), whom he had brought to Berlin in 1818, seemed always to be on the other, more conservative side, as were the king and his Lutheran copastor and University colleague Philipp Konrad Marheineke (1780–1846). There were similar problems with other closer colleagues as well. Nevertheless, he worked hard to settle disputes and continued to press for what he took to be right. By 1821 the theology students in Berlin numbered two hundred. Over the next decade this population climbed to more than six hundred, a height not reached again until the 1880s. During his twenty-six years about half of his courses were in New Testament exegesis. The rest were divided among courses in every part of theology, except the ancillary discipline of Old Testament, and philosophical subjects. Thus, he lectured on theological encyclopedia, Christian dogmatics, and ethics frequently and many times on the other areas of theology, notably church history and church statistics. He was the originator of practical theology. He also taught dialectic, history of philosophy, aesthetics, philosophical ethics, politics, and hermeneutics and criticism multiple times.

In the Berlin Academy of Sciences, to which he was inducted in 1810, he was a member of the philosophical and historical sections and a longtime secretary of the philosophy section. Before the Academy he gave fifty-three scholarly papers and addresses, ten of them on early Greek philosophers, most on major philosophical topics, and the rest on Academy concerns or memorials in public sessions (KGA I/11, 2002, 914).

Understandably, little time was left to put most of this intricately organized, well-argued lecture material into print—now, in somewhat limited fashion, the task of KGA II, beginning with an impressive 1,031-page volume of material on "The State" in KGA II/8 (1998). KGA I/14 (2003) contains a 768-page set of his shorter writings, most from this later period; likewise KGA I/9 (2003) presents a 721-page collection of his church-political writings.

In succession, he did manage to publish the following book-length works: *Brief Outline* (1811); revised 2nd edition (1830), a third collection of sermons (1814), the large critical study of *Luke* (1817), the lengthy essay on *Election* (1819), *The Christian Household* sermons (1820), the 1st edition of *Christian Faith* (1821–1822), the *Trinity* essay (1822), *Christian Festival Sermons* (1826), *On the Glaubenslehre* (1828), *Christian Faith* revised 2nd edition (1830–1831), the *Berliner Gesangbuch* (1830–1831), sermons in celebration of the handing over of the *Augsburg Confession* (1831), and a second collection of *Christian Festival Sermons* (1833). Many additional published theological essays are also included among the few noted here in the 732-page KGA I/10 (1990; see the Nicol translation of several, 2003).

With the numerous volumes of correspondence, all this and the KGA volumes of lecture and sermonic material yet to come comprise a sizeable output over this mere quarter of a century. How did Schleiermacher manage it? The short answer is: through extraordinarily clear-headed thought and discipline, virtually on a daily basis. The rest of the answer has to do with his open-ended but precisely worked out system of thought (illustrated in the concepts given in chapter 4) and with his attentive, intensive, diligent style of engagement in a wide circle of human affairs. Doubtless we should also add a question that points to his distinctively responsive, inventive person: who else, he must have thought, is going to do it? Current controversies and associated problems pressed relentlessly hard on him. There was little time to waste in fulfillment of his callings. As he constantly recommended to his students: one must work all these things out for oneself.

Free Sociality and the State

Thank God there was some regular surcease from his labors, some refreshment with his family and friends, in the cultural activities of Berlin, and in the free, relatively informal social exchange of the salons. In the latter neither church nor state could intervene. Participants had the privilege and challenge of interacting with other thoughtful persons whose gifts, ideas, and lifestyles differed but who were more or less equally committed to such exchange. Ideally—a goal toward which he worked in other domains—the state would become a constitutional, democratically principled supporter of both freedoms and equal rights for all, as would all other social institutions. He wrote about allied goals and processes repeatedly. As a subject of the king and would-be true citizen, during the war years he trained with the Berlin militia, and in the critical year of 1813 he edited a political newspaper from July through September and undertook a trip to the king's headquarters in Königsberg, from which he issued secret messages to Berlin.

After 1815, however, the king grew fearful of his political influence and had his preaching and lecturing closely monitored by the police so that Schleiermacher had to be very careful and circumspect in speaking about the state or he could lose everything. As a Christian, in all these domains one would find oneself acting not in accordance with ironclad rules belonging to each one but always in every domain and every moment as one who lives freely in relationship to God, as a continually repeating, lovingly correcting, faithfully generative, and authentically active presenter of God's reign. This latter expression of a Christian life is his most important legacy as an active participant in church, state, and society throughout all the later Berlin years.

Theology

In peculiar service of this vision, theology was indeed his chief *métier*, not just dogmatics however. As he describes the three parts of theology in *Brief Outline*, all of them, with their subdisciplines, form one interactive whole. All these disciplines—whether philosophically minded, historical, or practical—are indispensable to each other. All are rooted in faith, itself both grounded and expressed in feeling, not immediately in specific doctrinal beliefs or rules of conduct, as we will see laid out in chapter 2. Faith in a fuller sense is piety*, which includes thinking and acting thus rooted. Accordingly, he refers to "the faithful" with this meaning, not as "believers"; and "faith-doctrine" comes from the expression of "faith," not belief. Because of this basic orientation, Schleiermacher views all theological work as for leadership* among persons of faith and approaching faith, and he defines practical* theology as essentially "care of souls."

Influence

How has Schleiermacher the theologian been received?[23] In the nineteenth century he was received only minimally or in strong reaction, mostly because of his reputed historical-critical study of the Bible. Yet, among those who could read him in German, in the modern era as a whole, scarcely any area of theology has failed to be touched by his work—again whether by appropriation or by counterreaction based mostly on rumor alone or by ignoring genuine hermeneutical principles for understanding. Until the 1920s only a tiny few among his works were widely available in English. By 1960 I could detect obvious signs of a "renasence" in Schleiermacher studies in both Germany and North America (not yet in England then). This has continued to burgeon as scholars have come to realize at firsthand (a) how seminal his theological work was for our own work, (b) how richly useful were the numerous concepts he brought to theology from empirically grounded, philosophically minded inquiry (hence ch. 4 here), and (c) how much of a contemporary he is to us in our own efforts. Today this sense of the importance of the man and his works has begun to spread to other quarters of the world. Wherever his work is known, he is often prized for his contributions in philosophy—most notably in hermeneutical theory and practice and in his understanding of the art of doing philosophy altogether—as well as in theology, until recently his chief claim to fame. From here on, I concentrate on matters of religion, faith, and theology.

CHAPTER TWO

SCHLEIERMACHER'S PERSPECTIVE ON RELIGIOUS EXPERIENCE

If the feeling of absolute dependence, expressed as God-consciousness, is the highest stage of immediate self-consciousness, in that way it is also an essential element of human nature. No argument can be lodged against this claim based on the fact that for every human being there is a time when that element does not exist, for this is also a time when life is not yet complete. . . . We may imagine as great an interval as we like between two extremes, that of the most intimate sense of community and that of the faintest. . . . However, between these extremes we may also imagine it filled up by as many stages in between as we like.

—*Christian Faith* §6.3

An Opening Scene

Schleiermacher has taken a chair in his sitting room, to gather his thoughts on his primary subject: religion.[1] For two years he, now aged thirty, has been regularly settling in here by late evening to read his books and periodicals, to reflect on the day's events, often in correspondence, to meditate and think, and to write. A wood fire glows slightly, taking the chill off this fall night, but he is warmly dressed, expecting hours yet before dropping off to sleep for the roughly four hours to which he was accustomed. In semidarkness thus far, he has been gathering his thoughts to start a book, *On Religion*, as was his custom with sermons and essays from over the past ten years, pulling together its entire conception and design, often in a brief outline of notes before beginning anything and conjuring up the images and voices of his intended audience. Small of stature, quick of step, he strides across the room, ignites a candle-lit lantern at his desk, and draws a quill pen from a receptacle. It is a favored time, conducive to quiet contemplation*, for outside the clatter of carriages, hooves, and wagon wheels along the cobblestone streets has stilled and few sounds from other sources break the air. Out of the silence his thoughts whir, his emotions rise. Friedrich Schleiermacher leans his already naturally stooped shoulders over the tabletop and, for a moment, poises the pen over paper, then in a tiny script he states, almost mouthing the words under his breath:

The subject I propose to discuss has been massively denigrated by the very people from whom I especially claim a hearing. You may well wonder why I should make the attempt. Isn't it rather presumptuous for me to try to address people "exalted above the commonplace" and "imbued with the wisdom of our age" on the subject of religion? I must confess that I cannot readily anticipate winning your approval of my efforts— much less attain the more desirable goals of conveying my understanding and enthusiasm about the matter itself. When you stop to think about it, you realize that faith has never been everyone's affair. Only a few persons have ever seen what religion really is in any age, although millions have variously deluded themselves with the mere trappings of religion—with whatever happened to strike their fancy. But in our day especially, the self-styled life of cultured people hardly yields a glimpse of it. (*OR*, p. 39).

Preeminently, the individuals he addresses in these five systematically organized but rhapsodic discourses—openly personal, honestly direct, imaginative, and passionate— are many of the literati and aesthetes among his friends, also others whose echoes now resound throughout "enlightened" Germany, including some who are just inaugurating a new "romantic" movement partly in reaction. All are quite critical of religion. In the remaining four discourses* still other figures come to the fore, including those, to whom he here alludes, who falsely represent religion in their culture*, who ensnare the innocent in their perhaps well-meaning clutches. He continues:

> You no longer visit the temples of religion. Indeed, I am aware that for you it is just as *passé* to worship deity in the quiet sanctity of your hearts. Setting out the clever maxims of our learned men and the resplendent lines of our poets as wall decorations will do very well—but, please, nothing more "sanctimonious" than that! Suavity and sociability, art and learning, have won you over heart and soul—this no matter what little time or devotion you may give to them. These things dominate your lives so completely that no room is left for that eternal and holy being which, in your view, lies "beyond this world." As you look at the matter, you have neither any feeling for the supreme being nor any experience of it. I realize, moreover, how nicely you have succeeded in cultivating an earthly life so many-sided and magnificent that you "no longer stand in need of eternity." Having created an all-encompassing world for yourselves, you are too exalted to think about the source of your own creation. And I know you have made up your minds that nothing new or sound can be said about religion anymore. Sages and seers, not to mention scoffers and priests, have sufficiently covered the subject from every angle. You are inclined to acknowledge the testimony of priests least of all—that is plain to see. You have long since shunted them aside. You have declared them unworthy of your trust, since they seem fanatically attached to the crumbling ruins of their sanctuaries and cannot go on living even there without disfiguring and corrupting them still more. I am quite aware of all this. And yet, inwardly I feel I cannot help but speak. To me, what seems a divine impulse makes it impossible to withdraw my overture inviting precisely you, the cultured detractors of religion, to hear me out. (*OR*, pp. 39-40, *emphasis* added)

Schleiermacher did not use the word *critics** for this audience, for at that time the word *critic* stood chiefly for an activity that sought to correct ill-transmitted texts, after the model of philological criticism. However, in our lingo it forms an apt pair with *detractors* (*Verächtern*), for the people he had in mind were no fools, though sometimes they may have acted foolishly. They were earnest and rational in their detraction; they put well-thought-out alternatives on the well-trodden paths of whatever religion they were turning against. For Schleiermacher's mind the matter was dead serious and the societal-cultural-spiritual stakes were high.

As we have seen in chapter 1, both religion and its purported alternatives had occupied Schleiermacher's attention from childhood on. As soon as he had begun privately to try himself out as a writer a decade previously, he had started producing discourses on subjects of both kinds: Christian "religion," or "faith* and life," in sermons and more intellectual subjects, especially on morals, in essays available in both German and English translation today. In 1798 he had produced two large volumes of sermons by the great English pulpit orator Joseph Fawcett, in translation from English, his first publication.

In my view, Schleiermacher had already reached the outlook and maturity necessary to write *On Religion* before he arrived in Berlin in September 1796, when he had immediately become an active member of the budding circle of "early German romanticism" (as it came to be called). There can be no doubt, however, that this involvement, much of which occurred in evening conversations within the salons of abundantly cultured Jewish women, notably Rachel von Varnhagen and his close friend Henriette Herz was extremely stimulating to him. So was his demanding daily work as chaplain at Charité Krankenhaus (1796–1802), a general hospital alongside the river Spree, situated in an area near two main thoroughfares: the Friedrichstrasse and Unter den Linden. So was attendance at cultural events on or near the latter street, which was itself bordered by great palaces of the king's family and the Domkirche, where he had preached his examination sermon on Thursday, July 15, 1790, on "How One Must Be Constituted if One Is Truly to Repent and Improve." Within a few minutes one could walk to all these places from the Charité, where Schleiermacher talked with patients from all walks of life whose ailments, accidents, and mental breakdowns had brought them there and with whom he shared prayer and worship.

Manifestly, as a Christian pastor and theological thinker, Schleiermacher had profoundly internalized a continual process of receiving and then serving as a medium for the gifts of the Spirit. At the base of this process is what we would nowadays call "religious experience." In many respects, with this book *On Religion*, Schleiermacher, unbeknownst to himself and without including a single quantitative "empirical study," quickly became the most recognizable founder of the modern study of religion.

What Schleiermacher described in his book is a rather advanced phenomenon in human terms. At the same time, in its rudiments it is a general and almost inescapable human phenomenon at that more elevated level in which the experiences one may have had are then both reflectively, critically processed and outwardly enacted in a manner that serves to incite further inwardly felt experiences. My aim here is to offer my own account, which fortunately can still be couched very much in Schleiermacher's terms, of how these factors in mental functioning operate and grow. To capture more fully the feeling and perceiving aspects of mental functioning in their mediating role, I use what psychologists since William James and John Dewey have called "experience" in their stead. I refer to this process of experience as existing at an "advanced level" because people have to grow into it. In turn, this process of mental functioning has to become integrated into people's habits of thinking and acting before they can "grow" into a state of mind and heart (*Gemütszustände*) in which the process is a natural, comfortable feature of their lives.

Growth, we may note, is a summary term that John Dewey uses as a near synonym for *education*, defined in his great 1916 work *Democracy and Education* as "the continuous reconstruction of experience." The approach is part and parcel of Dewey's pragmatism, as I believe was true of Schleiermacher's educational theory before him. In his accounts of human existence, sometimes Dewey tends to dwell, perhaps overmuch, in the external precincts of experience, as may be seen in his theories of art* and educa-tion*. Accordingly, he tends to describe art more as craft than as expression of an inner state that is not clearly ascertainable until it finds formal expression. The same ten-dency appears in Dewey's account of "experience" in educational process, though, like William James, he is not so much a behaviorist as to ignore evidence of internal states.

Schleiermacher still has something highly important to contribute here in that his philosophical work overall affords a tighter integration of inner* and outer compo-nents in experience. That is to say, Schleiermacher more effectively views these two kinds of component as continually interactive and in a more consistent way. At this juncture, I simply wish to point out these general comparisons, which help to indicate why Schleiermacher's thought is still of considerable importance for current inquiry. Demonstration awaits other opportunities.

An Inner-Outer Dialectic

Basically, to "go through" an experience—or really to experience something—means to be an active recipient of it, to participate in it as part of an interaction. In other words, it is to be party to a *transaction* (a term Dewey sometimes uses). Therein meanings are born through an inner-outer dialectic* within or between self and oth-ers. Often in a transaction meanings are born through an implicit or explicit dialogue in which there are two or more members.

Whatever in the transaction is relatively external to the self is brought inward, usu-ally not in a simple one-time fashion but in what we might call an "oscillation" (a term Schleiermacher sometimes uses), a multiple back and forth processing of information. Psychoanalytic developmental theory defines this interactive process as, successively, "introjection," "projection," then "internalization," and, often still further, "identifica-tion" viewed as a kind of sharing and yet one that is to some degree distinctive to the self, edited as it were. Such theory also describes the staging of this process as one that sometimes occurs relatively slowly, moving successively through these three or four stages from introjection to internalization or identification over months or years. At other times the process occurs rather swiftly even in a given moment, reiterating the stages many times and in slightly differing editions. Such alterations of pace are read-ily to be seen or surmised in close observations of infants and young children, who eventually become adept at the process itself, in part moving through it unconsciously. At still other times individuals stop at a particular stage or they get stuck there or they regress to that point. All these variations, moreover, can happen at any time in the life cycle, depending on variable combinations of a person's internal states and circum-stances. Moreover, a particular person can learn to go through some iterations of the entire process quite consciously and intentionally, though generally people do not set out to do so. Individual persons can also form distinctive* patterns of relative recep-tivity* and relative self-active, spontaneous activity (Schleiermacher's distinction), though both are constantly going on, and, accordingly, the first two stages, which may occur many times before material is internalized, are inescapable. What I have just described constitutes the basic ebb and flow of human life, literally its ins and outs.

Although Schleiermacher did not have such detailed clinical language at hand, he understood the oscillating inner-outer quality of the process very well. When I first discovered this inner-outer dialectic in his thinking in my research on *Schleiermacher's Theological Method* (1961), I saw that it was of critical importance for understanding the nature of religion as he saw it and for grasping the structure of his doctrinal presentation as well. He knew quite well of the presence of this inner-outer dialectic in relations between human beings, between persons and other living things, between persons and inanimate objects, and between parts of oneself. Consequently, he often spoke of these twofold internal-external interactions. They lay at the very foundations of his presentation of the self as constituted interactively through and through, of the self as at once, interactively, body-mind/mind-body, and of perception and feeling as necessary roots of both thinking and action.

These interactions also gave him a powerfully informative way to account for the nature of religion, its development and its varied communal expressions. In particular, these manifestations of an inner-outer dialectic granted him a means to explain the self's appropriation of "God" as occurring in a relationship with and initiated by God. Thereby one is enabled to see the nature and presence of the divine as being revealed in and through the world, only there and chiefly in and through that part of the world in which human beings are present to one another. The inner-outer dialectic that is briefly described here is operative throughout this relationship as in all others that are possible for human beings. Finally, then, knowing about the manifestations of this dialectic enabled him to offer in his theological work an account, both devout and plausible, of how God is revealed* as accomplishing redemption* through the man Jesus* of Nazareth. Therein he could show that redemption is not only accomplished in what God once did through Jesus but that it is continually accomplished by God through communal* life and communication* wherein the start-off ministry* and presence of Jesus to other persons has actually been carried on "by the Spirit*" even though Jesus was no longer physically present.

In view of this account, it was not surprising to Schleiermacher that, given the rich diversity of historical conditions and of testimonies between and among distinctive selves and communities over time, what is carried forth from such a center would contain a certain oneness nonetheless. It also becomes clear why it was important for him to be able to compare and critique* but not summarily to dismiss expressions of faith* (relationships with God) different from his own in theology. This general understanding of human beings and of their diverse relationships with God helped make Schleiermacher a truly ecumenical theologian. For him, "speaking the truth in love," a motto for the full array of ministry in his eyes, did not entail rejecting all but one expression of truth*.

Anschauung and *Gefühl*—Once More

In this second of two main sections, I take up the theme of *Anschauung** and *Gefühl** yet again. Above I referred to this pair as mental functions, as bases and mediating agents for thinking and acting. The questions then arise: *Did Schleiermacher really mean this, and, for good or ill, did he not drop out* Anschauung *by the 1821 edition of* On Religion? Already in my longish 1961 dissertation on *Schleiermacher's Theological Method* I answered the first question with a resounding yes and the second question with a solid no accompanied with detailed explanations and proofs. I think, however, that I understand the two interlocking functions better now than I did then. In a long essay on "Schleiermacher's Conception" that I contributed to a sizeable multilingual volume on Schleiermacher's thought published in Italy (Olivetti, 1984), I reiterated these positions. At this point, I will in part briefly recapitulate the arguments that I already offered in these two works and in part add a newly organized reconstruction and analysis of what is involved in the choices Schleiermacher made, in large part affirming them as pertinent to present interests. In the process, I hope that I can better clarify these views in concise statements and with a minimum of additions from me.

The first thing to be shown is that grasping what Schleiermacher meant by this pair of concepts is essential for understanding how he intended to use them as mental functions in general, then as terms that help define religion. Here is my reconstruction, advanced in twelve steps.

1. Schleiermacher never dropped out *Anschauung* in the 1806 and 1821 editions of *On Religion*. In fact, as I have twice demonstrated and as any careful reader can see for oneself, several times he added the pair in contexts where they were not present in the original 1799 edition. Moreover, he did so in passages of major importance within the 1821 text. Thousands of bottles of ink have been spilled over this error, which has been perpetuated from one manuscript to another in a seemingly endless stream of so-called studies.

2. Schleiermacher took the trouble to emphasize the pair because they belong together, as will be demonstrated below.

3. It is true that in some contexts, early and late, Schleiermacher let the term *Gefühl* stand for both, I think for two reasons. First, in that feelings occur in the body, not only in the mind, and are sensed there, it stands to reason that they are at least initially responsive to something taken to be occurring in the external environment of the self or on occasion within the embodied self. Second, if this occurrence takes place only within the self, this does not necessarily make it merely internal to the feeling itself. In fact, I cannot imagine how this could ever be the case, and Schleiermacher did not suppose it could. There is always some relatively external referent or impact in relation to a given feeling, however unidentifiable it may be at a given moment, however vague or seemingly indeterminate the referent may turn out to be, and whether the origin is within the mind-body or not. To register the impression from without is the function of *Anschauung*.

4. In later years, Schleiermacher did occasionally replace or omit *Anschauung* in his texts, ostensibly because his meaning then was more likely to be confused with that of other well-known authors of the time. Likewise, he also occasionally replaced *God* and *universum* with other terms such as *Gottheit* ("deity," "godhead") or "the Highest" and with *Weltall* ("world in its entirety"), respectively. This maneuvering did not mean that he dumped the first meanings or ceased to use the corresponding words altogether. Frequently, in fact, he kept them just as they were.

In any case, it does not matter whether some use of *Anschauung* by Kant or somebody else has been rendered as "intuition" in translation or whether the translation was correct in those instances. For Schleiermacher, *Anschauung* is indeed always a relatively internal phenomenon, because it is an internal mental function that registers what comes into the sensorium from relatively external sources, including the body.

Nevertheless, the referent is always external relative to any given affective state. This is why the most frequent, ordinary uses of *Anschauung* must be translated "perception," as they tend to be wherever the word is placed.

In this connection a particular problem arises, namely that *Wahrnehmung* also means "perception," but that term does not have the levels of meaning that *Anschauung* does, so I always use "sense perception" for *Wahrnehmung*. Only in very odd cases would we say that "red" is "intuited." Normal usage, in any modern Western language at least, would demand the word *perceived*. That is the ordinary meaning of the word *perceive*, whether it is found in Schleiermacher's text as *Wahrnehmung* or *Anschauung*, and the words are meant to stand for those respective mental functions. This is why Schleiermacher chooses to pair the word with *Gefühl* (feeling).

5. We may stop for a minute to recognize that language can be tricky. For example, in French the usual word for "feeling" is *sentiment*, but that word does not mean "sentiment" in English, as in "gushy sentiment." It refers, rather, to a sensory phenomenon held in the body. By extension, we say such things as "I feel that such and such," but we know that the expression is in itself truncated. That is to say, we mean that we hold the belief with some degree of feeling, the index of which depends on our spoken inflection or on our adding an adjective such as "strongly" to "feel." In French one would probably not ordinarily say "I have the feeling (*sentiment*) that you should . . ." but would simply say "I think that" (*je pense que*), just as we normally, and with greater correctness, do in English.

6. To return to the mainstream of our argument, a close study of Schleiermacher's texts shows that he has several levels of usage for the word *Anschauung*. Virtually always, the context tells us which it is.

The lowest, simplest usage, and the easiest not to mistake, is mere "perception," here a close synonym for *Wahrnehmung* and thereby very closely tied to "sensation" (*Empfindung*). In ordinary usage perceptions are easily discriminated from sensations, and so in German, as in English, there are different words for them. When *Anschauung* is used at that level, to "perceive" is literally "to look upon" (*anschauen*) something. Almost always, the "something" is "out there." Sometimes the object is close to home, as it were; it is then actually in or of one's own body. I can perceive or sense that there is a twitch in my leg or that my cheek is very warm (maybe I am blushing), or I may not be able to locate the object, though it is within me and there are sensations in my body that point to it (maybe I am anxious or fearful).

To skip intermediate levels for the moment, I can also have a rather complex kind of *Anschauung*, namely *Anschauung des Universums*. At this point, the language can get confusing, particularly when one tries to translate. Certainly, in using this phrase Schleiermacher intends to refer to looking upon the universe taken as a whole, not gazing at the starry skies. That is why he uses the Latin word *universum* (which, by the way, is also a proper English word, though rarely used now). He does not mean "world*" in any of its ordinary uses. He means the entire world, everywhere, on and beyond Earth. As he explains, he means further to refer to the entire *Naturzusammenhang*, the interconnectedness* of nature as a whole*, including all animate nature.

So, how do we manage to look upon, or perceive, the entirety of nature in all its complex interconnectedness? Well, we "gain a perspective" on it that takes all of it into account. As an inclusive orientation of our thoughts this perspective might be captured in the term *Weltanschauung*, or "world view." Suppose, however, that Schleiermacher wishes to stick more closely to the root sense of *Anschauung* here, as I am quite sure he does. Do we have a way to render that entirely comprehensive experience of the whole interconnectedness of nature that he indicates? Here the translator must choose: stick to the root word *perception* or choose another way of speaking.

Intuition might work, though we would rarely if ever say "intuit red," but both ordinary and academic uses of *intuit* refer to a rather vague and indefinable, mysterious, extraordinary, and even arcane grasp of something, so that situation provides a strong reason not to use it here. Schleiermacher would not apply any of these qualities to the phrase. He means a clear, straightforward apprehension of the universe as it is taken to be, in all its comprehensiveness. A patina of awe and wonder cling to the phrase, one such that perhaps no word in another language would bear a sound that would convey it, certainly not in English. So, we must do what we can. What about something like gain or have "a perspective on the universe" or on "the universum" or on "the universe in its entirety"? That's as far as I have been able to get.

7. In between these two levels there are further usages of the pair *Anschauung* and *Gefühl*. Eventually Schleiermacher did often split the pair up. My analyses show that he did so for purposes of clarity and convenience only. The sense of their importance as a pair, particularly at the level where he is referring to religious experience, never left him.

Let us try to take the two members of the pair separately, as Schleiermacher sometimes did, referring them, first of all, not to religious experience as such but to their general relations to thinking and acting. Immanuel Kant claimed that "there is nothing in the mind not first in the senses." Certainly, in order to function in a general way our minds depend on our capacities for sensation. Whether that is always true is open to dispute. In any case, perception functions at the very least to mediate between what is contained in our sensations and in our thinking and acting. Moreover, most observers would say that there is no such thing as pure sensations or sense data unmediated by perception and thus not changeable by perception when it figures into other mental functions such as thinking. Now, thinking with the aim of knowing* is a major kind of thinking (dialectic* is about that) and thinking with an aim to act morally is another kind (ethics* is about that, and Schleiermacher borrows an even broader meaning as well, one that refers to all human conduct). Probably, when Schleiermacher refers to perception as a basis for thinking, he is normally considering not so much all forms of thinking as especially those two kinds.

If we amend the above statement to read "there is no such thing as an uninterpreted fact," we can readily conceive of perception as operating at even higher levels than that on which it mediates sensation. These levels would be of mounting complexity of input into interpretation, even beyond the already complex level wherein we try to understand exactly what another person means (all this is what hermeneutics* is about). That is to say, banking on one's perceptions and gathering or even revising some of them to serve purposes of, successively, rough opinion formation, carefully considered opinion formation, and attaining to something approaching "pure reason" would take us to many distinguishable levels of perception, defined not only by uses of the word but also by what goes into the content of perception itself. At the higher reaches, then, perception is unmistakably affected by factors beyond sensation. At such points, various sorts of thought also affect perception, including thought that serves to form certain kinds of associations (verbal, metaphorical, and so on) and thought that serves to integrate divers materials, for example. A *Weltanschauung* would be a general outlook on the world so affected.

8. Now, "presupposition*," a phenomenon of mental functioning to which Schleiermacher often adverts, is a function in which the influence of perception and thinking on each other can go both ways, and it, too, exists at various levels. One notable example is that of the notion of causality*. For centuries, the idea of causality as action from a distance was widely held and even became a matter of unconscious presupposition, which made it very difficult to access critically*. In introducing the idea of "divine causality*" into *Christian Faith* Schleiermacher rejected that older concept, which had long been presupposed in Christian discourse and is still often present today. In referring to *Anschauung* and *Gefühl* as a baseline experience from which thinking and acting may proceed in the religious life, Schleiermacher wishes us to imagine a level that is relatively presuppositionless. He no doubt realized that this level of mental functioning can never be absolutely so, but it is far more nearly pure in that respect than doctrine or morals, which rather refer back to them. Do transformations of doctrine and morals affect them in turn? Yes. We live in history, thus we cannot escape that wide circling of influence. This is particularly true with respect to *Anschauung*, which can function at so many different levels.

9. In contrast, it might seem difficult to place feeling at so many different levels. Yet, Schleiermacher did discriminate between a few levels of feeling, depending, in these cases, on their sources and on their objects of reference. My analyses of his usage lead me to distinguish between three levels of special significance.

The bottom level, as it were, contains pangs of physical pleasure or lack of pleasure (*Unlust* is the term used by both Schleiermacher and Freud). Although it is customary to refer to these as things we feel, and there is little likelihood of that practice changing, they may be thought of as mere sensations. They are very different from delight or taking pleasure in, also from pain (since the lack of pleasure does not entail pain) or displeasure at.

Another level, far removed, includes moods and other sustained affective states such as anxiety or depression or anger that can be quite negative, though they are not necessarily so, but also sustain unquestionably positive character traits, strengths, and virtues, such as love, joy*, peace, patience, and kindliness. All of these states are more complex in their makeup and are less discrete in the directions they take. They cover a great many situations, and they can underlie strong tendencies to thought and action. People are perhaps less accustomed to attaching feelings of this sort to such matters as mathematics or science, but it cannot be hard to imagine that other complex feelings affect one's predilections and choices there as well.

Schleiermacher's analysis implies the view that no thinking or acting is affect-free or can be rightly conceived as unaffected by feelings of some kind. There is generally little sense of this truth for two principal reasons that I can think of. First, the difficulties that passions can get people into have led to a denigration of passion in a majority of cultures or areas of culture*, especially where "reason" rides high, and feelings are treated as if they ride on the coattails of passion. Second, as yet there is no widespread knowledge of how the emotional aspects of life develop and no clear stage theory of affective development.

I believe, on the basis of clinically based studies of development in general and of reflections on familiar behavior in fictional literature and elsewhere, that affective development can be specified in detail. In fact, a few clinical theorists have attempted initial formulations of such an account, and many people can identify such phenomena as road rage to be infantile and can identify more specifically and limitedly articulated expressions of anger as relatively quite mature, and so forth. However, cognitive, behaviorist, and quantitative interests hold such a powerful hegemony over psychological and social sciences today, even over the reigning theories of education and child development, that there is scarce room for these other attempts to thrive.

Schleiermacher himself was far from having such an account, even speculatively*. He did take great care not to confuse the two kinds of level indicated above with religious feeling as such, though he realized that they were bound to participate in expressions of religious feelings such as love and joy, more or less appropriately. This, I think, is why he tried to single out what is distinctive about and defining of religious feeling in a formula.

10. Accordingly, in *Christian Faith* Schleiermacher coins two conceptual phrases for the purpose. The first concept is that of "immediate religious self-consciousness*," which refers to a feeling of a particular kind. The second concept refers to that specific kind of feeling as "the absolute feeling of dependence*," which can characterize even lower stages of religious development such as fetishism or polytheism, where the feeling of dependence, of utter and overwhelming influence from a source outside oneself, is manifested in an exclusive but limited direction and is held to without reservation. This feeling may eventually rise for some people, notably in the context of monotheistic religions, where the divine is seen to be omnipotent and omnipresent, as "the feeling of absolute dependence." That is, there one finds oneself to be in relationship with the Supreme Being*, in a world wherein everything is indissolubly interconnected, wherein one is oneself utterly embedded in the whole*.

This feeling, he claims, is variously expressed in the numerous varieties of monotheistic religions. Moreover, he would also seem to hold that the feeling could be found in some nontheistic consciousness as well, as he intimates both in *On Religion* and wherever he speaks of "God" as not simply "a being," on the pattern of human beings. Within Christianity* itself, this feeling is not static and is not, therefore, to be simply taken for granted. It is a feeling that can mature. It is an ideal, to be sure, but one that can be approximated variously within Christianity and that can be used as a norm and critical standard for doctrine within communities of faith.

This is how recognition of the feeling of absolute dependence is used throughout Schleiermacher's systematic presentation of doctrines in *Christian Faith*. This norm and critical standard is not itself propositional; it is experiential, not doctrinal. In this book, it represents the baseline experience of *Anschauung* and *Gefühl* within a given community of faith regarding their relationship to God*, whose redeeming action in Jesus the Christ* has been carried forward by the divine Spirit* from Jesus' ministry to the disciples and others around him to that present community of faith. In this case, the community of faith is the Evangelical* churches in Germany at that time, so it is no universal feeling that Schleiermacher refers to.

11. Now we are in a position to put the two terms *Anschauung* and *Gefühl* back together. The content of *Christian Faith* makes quite clear, despite all the subsequent confusion over word selection that I have mentioned, that the feeling of absolute dependence, viewed as a completely religious feeling, has an object. That object is God and God's entire, wholly interconnected process of creating and preserving the world. Nothing is extraneous to that referent, that object of faith. This faith is itself a relationship to the living God. God is alive, at work redeeming the world through the Redeemer and therein by the Spirit, viewed as the "common spirit" that both indwells the church and by its power extends beyond the church* into the rest of the world. Continually, the relationship with God that exists in faith is an experience of existing in relation to God. It is "an immediate existential relationship," as Schleiermacher states. Fundamentally it is an experience of being utterly dependent, of being interconnected with the whole of the entire created and sustained process of nature, including the history of human beings, in and through which God's grace* is made manifest.

This experience has two aspects to it. First, it is inseparably God's own being and action, perceived above all in the ongoing community of people by which God's redeeming activity in Christ is made known. There is no other medium through which to know God, as if God could be known *in se*, independently in Godself. The experience is one of God's unhalting love* or grace* and therefore, and only then, because of human beings' need of redemption. Sin* itself Schleiermacher describes as that state in which God's grace has aroused the sense of the need for redemption. This is the *Anschauung* aspect, the perception of God's grace and, correspondingly, of humanity's sin.

The second aspect is that of *Gefühl*, of feeling as the fundament of people's faithful relationship with God. Therein God's inseparable nature and action, "the one eternal divine decree*" of God's creative activity rising to redemption, is felt. It is felt in all the corresponding ways that Christian doctrines are meant faithfully to capture and Christian morals are meant faithfully to enact. In this way, the combination of perception and feeling serves to mediate—by what God through the historical Jesus as the Redeemer has set in motion and God's Spirit is continuing to make possible—between what God has done and is yet to do. Experience, viewed as the combination of perception and feeling, is the base. The rest is chiefly thinking and acting, each of which is to be imbued with that experience and judged in terms of correspondence with it.

12. Schleiermacher had always said that *Anschauung* and *Gefühl* are two distinguishable aspects of the same thing, inseparable from and indispensable to each other. In religious experience, therefore, without *Anschauung* there is nothing for feeling to be about, and without *Gefühl* there is nowhere for perception to go in the life of faith. Outside that life, the two still have basic and mediating functions, moving directly to thought and action. The latter two activities, however, obtain a tie to religious experience and a critical standard from it only when distinctly religious experience is their sole referent, else Christian doctrine and ethics would degenerate into something dryly rational and/or into something magical* in their operating purely supernaturally*,

beyond the conditions of God's own world*. In the end, then, Christian thinking would not authentically look to Christian action, nor would Christian action authentically arouse Christian thought. The experience of faith itself, constituted as it is by appropriately religious perception and feeling, enables genuinely free and fruitful interaction between the two.

Concluding Remarks

I have sought to keep this entire reconstructive account as close to Schleiermacher's language usage, presentation, and arguments as possible. Only in a few places, notably in using distinctions from advanced descriptions of child and adult development and in choosing a few terms allied to Schleiermacher's terms, though not identical with them, have I stretched slightly beyond what he thought or directly implied. Moreover, I have done this purely for the sake of clarifying, in short compass, what he actually said and to obviate misunderstanding. As may well be evident by now, I believe that his understanding of what I call "basic experience" as comprised by *Anschauung* and *Gefühl*, is powerfully efficacious. It is most notably, but not exclusively, so in its recognizing authentically religious and Christian content in people's lives.

Of course, in their mediating function, the basic religious experience contained in this interlocking pair of mental functions also leads to other, hopefully authentic levels of faith experience in thought and action. This will happen, Schleiermacher would claim, only if they are made subject to the critical standard afforded by that originative, basic experience. Thus, I have given an account of *experience*, already a favored though often misused term in English, in such a way that it would be consistent with Schleiermacher's views.

Schleiermacher himself tended to use the word *experience* (*Erfahrung*) in the same broad sense that is customary in English as well, at its root referring to anything one may undergo or go through. There is also an English use of the word that has been unreflectively applied to his theory of religion, one that interprets experience as purely or chiefly subjective*, without any clear objective reference. This attribution to what has been set forth here concerning his understanding of the pair *perception* and *feeling* is plainly mistaken. In view of that frequent error, I have taken pains to distinguish the basic "experience" that he quite clearly represents in the pair from more complex, highly complex, and mediated experience. Yet, it too is both subjective and objective in content, irretrievably so. As I see it, the mistake of branding Schleiermacher's outlook as subjectivist is not a linguistic artifact, however. It derives from poor reading and from slavish attachment to what others have said. Only then does the application of *experience* to Schleiermacher's approach become sloppy usage. Thus, my attempt here has been to clarify what he meant and thereby to save a perfectly apt term from misuse. Along the way, I trust that it has become apparent that to develop the habit of reading for accuracy one must get accustomed to expecting several levels of usage for some terms. Schleiermacher's discourse especially demands this habit.

Now, before bringing the present chapter to an end, we may notice another, closely allied example of serious mistakes that poor reading and inexact attention to linguistic usage can lead to. In Schleiermacher's book *On Religion*, the second of five discourses considers what he calls *das Wesen der Religion*. Repeatedly, *das Wesen* has been read as "the essence," as if everything else among the five discourses were either purely introductory (I) or relatively secondary (III–V). Sorry. I hate to seem harsh in countering such a time-honored tradition, but this reading is plain wrong. An "essence" is distilled, leaving dross; it is at the core, as distinguished from surrounding tissue or the periphery; it is the necessary and sufficient marker, in comparison with which all else is either unnecessary for a definition or insufficient or both; it is the real, solid substance versus mere and variable attributes.

None of these meanings carries what Schleiermacher was doing in the book. He starts off (I, "Apologia") by characterizing the critics of or detractors against religion, some but not nearly all of them "despisers" (not the only or the most accurate English meaning for *Verächter* in this context, as he describes it). Then (II, "The Nature of Religion") he gets right to the heart of the matter, indicating in a very focused way how *religion* has become for many a substitute word for *morals* or for sets of cognitions or beliefs, and he uses these contrasts to lay out in great detail what religion does consist of. The word for what it consists of is *Wesen*, a perfectly good German word for "nature of." Admittedly, it can sometimes be used (mostly because of other habits in the history of Christian philosophy) in the alternative ways I have listed above. However, in relation to God Schleiermacher never uses the term in these alternative ways. Likewise, here it is quite clearly used to discuss "the nature of religion," what it is.

He never stops doing this in the remaining discourses. He asks: *Does religion develop?* Yes, and some of that can readily, if provisionally, be mapped out (III). *Does religion, when regarded in and of itself, have communal features?* Yes, unexceptionably so (IV). *Finally, does religion possess historical variety and widely present itself in many kinds?* Again, yes, and that produces a nearly intractable problem, not least because so-called religions contain features that are not authentically religious, that are but excrescences posing under the guise of religion, but meanwhile we can form positive attitudes and expectations in facing that mixed reality (V).

Given the diverse phenomena of religion to be seen, Schleiermacher could have started with the fifth discourse (as William James did) and worked his way back through the discourses as they were actually arranged. Then, however, he would have had to do much backfilling and preliminary explaining along the way. The direction he took was clearer, less cluttered. As his mode of presenting the successive discourses makes quite clear, it was all done in order to give an account of what religion is, its nature. The work is so astonishingly fresh in part because of what he lays down in the second discourse. Religion is so plainly distinguishable from the descriptions that critics or detractors typically attach to it, not infrequently identifying problems that are to be found in actual religions as far as surface appearances are concerned. Occasionally even adherents make the same mistakes, and so he sometimes refers to their misinterpretations as well. Look beneath the surface, he urges. When you do that, you will be able to see the surface itself with much greater discrimination. Then, and only then, will you be in a position to grasp that within religion and all its developments and communal expressions which most suits you at base, perhaps draws you to it because of life forces already at work in you. Schleiermacher never leaves this one complex theme regarding the nature of religion, never in any of the three editions. In his revisions he only strives to address this theme with greater clarity and adequacy.

In the end, I find that this same impetus has driven me as well, in the face of two centuries of previous response. I hope that new readers of Schleiermacher's discourses on the nature of religion, as of his works on Christian theology, will be of a mind to read more carefully than has often been done. The effect, I am sure, will repay the effort. Of course, all interpretations are subject to revisions, my present one included, but I have tried to offer you an accurate, well-grounded one.

When Schleiermacher stepped away from his writing desk, manuscript in hand, he had, in effect, created a new era in religious thought. This had occurred before he turned to the field of theology five years later. His discourse on religion was indeed rhapsodic at this point. However, it already repeatedly issued from profound, philosophically minded[2] reflection of the sort we have seen here, all drawn from a base experience of religion, or faith, itself. The same procedures and qualities would become evident as pastor Schleiermacher later entered lecture halls at the University to be founded in that same city in 1808–1810.

Questions for Reflection

Do you find this account of religious experience helpful for your own purposes? Does it click with your own experience? If not, where do you think Schleiermacher, or I, might have stumbled? How might the account be repaired?

CHAPTER THREE

A SYSTEMATIC SUMMARY OF SCHLEIERMACHER'S THEOLOGY

Nothing is more irreligious than to demand general uniformity among humanity. Likewise nothing is more unchristian than to seek uniformity in religion.

—*On Religion, 321*

Having briefly told Schleiermacher's story in chapter 1, including his extraordinarily creative effort in fathering modern theology, and having outlined his basic understanding of religious experience in chapter 2, we now proceed to a brief systematic summary of Christian doctrine and ethics produced for the church in his theological work in Berlin. This summary is ordered in seven successive parts: God, the New Life in Christ, Election and the Holy Spirit in the Church, the Shared Ministry of Clergy and Laity, Revelation, the Triune God, and Christian Ethics. I invite you to consult chapter 4 as you work through these rather densely packed pages to find clarifying definitions. Moving within the context of the Evangelical* Church of his time, Schleiermacher takes Christian experience to be based fundamentally on a consciousness of God and thereby lodged in a relationship with God. Thus, it is appropriate to begin and end with his doctrine of God, a procedure quite contrary to what most of his critics expect of him. One could almost as well begin with Christ, since Christ's consciousness of God enables all the rest, but in the end Schleiermacher's "theology" is all about God's activity in and through ourselves and the world. In particular, his entire system of doctrine is about God. The other six categories could be placed in any order.

God

What is the nature* of God*? First of all, in Schleiermacher's view Christian religious consciousness presupposes that the divine* presence, the being and will of which is revealed* in Christ*, is the one power by which the entire universe* is created and preserved. Further, this view is presupposed* because of the way God's presence is fundamentally experienced by faithful* Christians: that God is almighty and all-knowing. (More about these characteristics later.) Moreover, this one, indivisible God is manifest as Spirit* in the spirits of Christian women, men, and children. In that this spiritual presence is proclaimed* and shared within Christian community*, God comes to be known precisely as that one Spirit, available to all human beings whether acknowledged or not.

To speak in personal* terms, through the unfolding of Christ's own God-consciousness*, this one God, the creator and preserver of all things, is deemed to be actual among us in the church* and thereby in each individual. God is not an individual, not a person, but through the passage in history of Christ's God-consciousness and his corresponding words and deeds God exists in vital relationship with us as persons, just as God is efficaciously active in fulfillment of God's own purposes, of God's one eternal divine decree*, in ways appropriate to the rest of creation. God is seen not to be bound by time or space. God is infinite, not finite, not limited or restricted, in dealings with the creation. By the same token, God is eternal, not bound by the conditions of time. As such, God is also not limited or restricted by the contrasts* that inevitably appear in nature* and thought, such as that between good and evil*. Yet, God can be felt, known, and actively accompanied by us in ways proper to us as human beings. God also uses the rest of creation to realize purposes that stretch from the point at which the universe came into being into the indefinite future, beyond all that we can humanly know or expect.

Thus, God is sovereign and supreme over nature, is supernatural* and in no sense identical with it. However, God is also experienced as coming to us only in and through the wholly interconnected* world* of nature. God becomes present to us, is revealed* and made known, only through this "economy." What God brings into our lives, in vital relationship, is not an infusion of something direct or unmediated from outside the conditions of nature, including human nature. Thus, we can know nothing of what God is outside those conditions. This is why the incarnation* of God's Spirit in Christ is of critical importance for Christian faith*. Among Christians, the exercise of God's grace* for the redemption* of all is seen to occur by means of this crucial event in history. All else that involves this redemptive presence of God is but preparatory* for and subsidiary to this event, which continues in and through the church.

The visible church is not itself the Redeemer, but the Redeemer is now visibly present in the whole world, notably and ideally in and through the visible church. To say, therefore, that Christ continues to dwell among us through the succession of generations since Jesus* was alive is exactly the same thing as to say that the Holy Spirit* indwells the church as its common spirit. Insofar as there are signs of Christ's presence beyond the visible, institutional church, God's redemptive Spirit is there as well. One day, we may expect, though we do not know altogether how, that this Spirit, thus described, will dwell in all. No one will be left behind, no matter when they have lived on this earth. Because of the proclamation* and living out of this good news from the time of Christ onward, it no longer has to be a mystery* that God's eternal will and decree would be eventually to achieve redemption for all in Christ and by the Holy Spirit, which, as we have affirmed, consist in one and the same process and outcome. The only remaining mystery is precisely how God has been and is and will be achieving all this, and that, we may say in faith and love and hope, may surely be left to God. We Christians are but witnesses. We are not called* to be the bearers of full, certain knowledge regarding the mystery of God.

What, then, can be said of the attributes of God, thus revealed? Can anything really be said with any surety? Is it all a matter of subjectivity*? What is known of God through the religious consciousness of a Christian is not merely subjective. For one thing, it is consensually confirmed. For another, it is about this one God, whose presence in relationship with us is immediately felt. So is our absolute, unqualified, unreserved, and utterly all-encompassing feeling* concerning our dependent relation to the entire interconnectedness of nature in and through which we find ourselves to exist in Christ and find God to exist in and for and with us in Christ—individually, socially, and as a species*. These feelings are all intertwined and interdependent. They all point to an objective reality, one not in any way dependent on our subjective states but on which we are, in contrast, dependent. Because of our experience in faith and not because of any separable, prior, so-called rational, or natural theology, whatever we are enabled to state as Christians concerning God must derive purely from this actual relationship with God. It cannot come from any other source. To the faithful, moreover, this is the fullest, most supreme and sure objective reality we can know.

Now, every proposition concerning Christian faith and life is about God—that is, about God's relationship to self and world in the context of Christian community. That Schleiermacher has chosen to distinguish among three types of proposition (CF §30)—God, self, and world—in his account of Christian faith from an Evangelical* point of view is for the sake of convenience alone. They all refer to different aspects of that same relationship. The three sections on divine attributes in *Christian Faith* summarize what being in that relationship tells us about God-with-us, through the world and in redemption. With respect to divine grace, then, these attributes are themselves all summed up in the pair divine love and wisdom. (See just below.) With respect to sin or the need for redemption or a lack of relationship with God, the designated attributes are another pair that affirm God to be holy and just. Schleiermacher's systematic presentation takes up sin first but with the explanation that Christians grasp the full meaning of sin* only once they have grasped God's grace*—that is, only in the process of regeneration* (being reborn to new life in Christ) and sanctification* (receiving blessedness* from God in their ongoing life, day by day), in short, being redeemed as the need for redemption is overcome. Finally, presupposed in Christian consciousness of all this is the claim that the God who at once and inseparably both wills and acts for the redemption of all human beings is the very same as the One God who creates and preserves the universe and thus has the attributes of omnipotence and omniscience. In Schleiermacher's analysis, what God wills God does, and what God accomplishes is precisely identical with what God eternally intends, without being limited or conditioned by space and time.

Through painstaking critical examination of numerous alternative accounts of divine election, or predestination, of human beings to salvation, he finds any account that affirms or implies a double predestination to heaven or hell, salvation or damnation, to be drastically faulty. This is so either logically speaking or because the claims and arguments used limit God's foreknowledge and power without warrant. The rubric he sometimes employs to capture all of this is "the one eternal divine decree*," which through Christ and the ongoing activity of the Holy Spirit both aims at and decisively accomplishes the redemption of humanity. God's creating beings possessed of free* will makes the path to full and final redemption difficult, but it does not defeat God's purpose.

In God, what is wisdom, then? It is that order and sense by which God governs the world. Already in his extensive "notes" for lectures on philosophical ethics in 1804–1806, Schleiermacher described wisdom and love as "the inner roots of moral development" (*Ethics*, 201). There he wrote: "Everything we have seen as existing, according to its form in wisdom, attains an identity of being and becoming. Moreover, wisdom like love goes beyond moral action" (153; cf. 156-58, 162, also 207). I have indicated that this formulated pair of potencies in his early ethical writings, which always persisted in his thinking, is due to his religious sensibility as evidenced in his "teleological*" account of Christianity and in his use of the pair to present the culminating attributes of wisdom and love in *Christian Faith* (Tice, op. cit., 177).

If he had desired to provide a mere exposition of Christian faith instead of the carefully ordered, critical mode of argument he adopted, Schleiermacher could well have begun by laying out the triform understanding of the one God revealed in Christ, which he did roughly follow, in any case, in part 1 and then part 2, finally moving to the fundamental character of divine activity summarized in *Christian Faith* §§164-69, namely the divine love and wisdom. Here is a summary of what he sets forth there.

The Christian's "consciousness of communion with God" in redemption, the object of which is "the planting and extension" of the church, is traced to "the divine* causality," described as "the divine government* of the world," which is expressed as divine love and wisdom (CF §§164-65). The reigns of nature and of grace in which God governs are "fully at one" (*völlig eins*) and are disclosed as "the revelation* of God in the flesh" (§164.1). In this perspective, everything in both physical and human nature would have been different were it not for this divine decree of redemption through Christ and in the community of faith by the Holy Spirit. Before that turning point in history all was "preparatory and introductory," and afterward all is a matter of "development and fulfillment" (§164.2).

Now, in this divinely ordered process, the "will," "tendency," or "disposition" of God is God's love, while the "acting on" God's intention, the "ordering of the entirety of them," and the "art" of doing so or of "realizing" God's love is God's wisdom (§165.1). Thus, in the work of redemption all divine self- communication is perfectly and absolutely realized in accordance with these two attributes (§165.2).

In the redemptive process, what is especially worked on then? It is humanity's "God-consciousness*," which underlies piety*. It is not focused on individuals as such, in isolation from that whole*. In this light, it is of key importance to recognize, in a way wholly in keeping with the New Testament, that ultimately no other attribute but love can be predicated of the Supreme* Being with full warrant, and also that, in this regard, love alone, with its enactment by divine wisdom, even among those others called attributes discussed in parts 1 and 2 of this treatise, is totally equivalent to the Supreme Being, to God as Godself. No other attributes, therefore, can be substituted for the name *God*. The others are wholly about how God operates in the world. Even the status of wisdom is indirect and derivative in our consciousness compared with love, though it is carried along with love in that the two are taken to be inseparable (§§167.1-2).

With regard to wisdom, the world is seen to be "an absolutely harmonious divine work of art," in which God's "absolute, . . . perfect self-presentation and communication" is engaged. This activity, in turn, gradually becomes for us "a complete presentation of the almighty love of God." In this activity, moreover, there can be no distinction between choice of ends and means, for there are no means outside what God has brought forth (§168.1). Again, with wisdom everything is related to God's "revelation*" in redemption, God's new creation and God's election of all human beings in Christ (§168.2). In this light, the world is seen to be good. From this perspective, however, nothing salvific is to be expected from the nonconscious, nonrational domains of this world. "Hence," in conclusion, "the world can then be grasped as a complete revelation of divine wisdom only insofar as the Holy Spirit makes itself felt as the ultimate world-forming power from the Christian church outward" (§169.3).

This first systematic summary of a major theme in Schleiermacher's theology is derived from the entire system of doctrine that he deems to be genuinely reflective of Evangelical faith and sufficient for its common life. Most of the material positions of the work from which the summary is chiefly taken are critical* in form and content. That is, the discourse painstakingly considers alternative statements both from Christian tradition and from contemporary theologians, and it runs through arguments that have been offered for each one. As he proceeds he attempts to distill a clear understanding of the faith-propositions that he has chosen to articulate within the closely interconnected sections of the systematic presentation as a whole. In due course, he also makes clear how and why he eschews both a tightly closed system that is formed deductively and a loose loci presentation, in which various traditional doctrinal statements are exposited in an array of positions accompanied by rejections of alternative views without the careful historical-critical attention Schleiermacher gives them. In his discourse no rationalist position is to be found, nothing of the web of speculations* familiar among many of his contemporaries, made up of ideas and arguments drawn from outside Christian faith itself, either to explain or to justify it. Strictly supernaturalist* positions are also missing—the other chief alternative to what he was doing. The supernaturalists have typically held that no natural, empirically* describable means are involved in the events of divine revelation and redemption. These events literally come down from above, though often they presuppose an original divine verbal inspiration of scripture that is authentically carried forth through preaching and theological exposition of this "word*." Schleiermacher, too, affirms an originative authority in Holy Scripture, but his understanding of what this crucial aspect of the church's creeds and confessions means is quite different. Both types of alternative positions concerning God, revelation*, and inspiration of the word were present in sixteenth- and seventeenth-century Protestant orthodoxy, as they are very much in evidence today. Among inheritors of the eighteenth-century Enlightenment in his day, so were various "liberal" interpretations of scripture and tradition—if noticed very much at all—that philosophize, empiricize, sociologize, and spiritualize onetime Christian content in ways that are scarcely recognizable, as is also true today. Schleiermacher, though authentically "liberal" in his thinking, would have nothing to do with these approaches either. In his theological work he wants to speak of God, revealed in Christ, not of these other things. These distinctively Evangelical orientations in his thinking will also become more evident as we proceed to other major themes.

Questions for Reflection

The concept love, when applied to God, is simply the most focused, purposeful way of pointing out God's caring and good pleasure as the initial, continually efficacious, and ultimate world-shaping power. It is the principle that both sets off and sustains all that is good in the world and overcomes the temporary ravages of sin. There has been much contention regarding whether such a reduction of all God's attributes to love can work and as to whether this can constitute a true knowledge of God. Certainly this conclusion is not immediately obvious. It has taken Schleiermacher much historical-critical effort to achieve this synthesis. At this point, to what extent does the overall view seem plausible to you? Would you want to propose some alternative? If so, on what grounds?

The New Life in Christ

As the Christ*, the Redeemer*, the most important thing to say about Jesus* of Nazareth, in Schleiermacher's view, is that he lived. In itself his death may bear redemptive overtones, as it were, but it is not a necessary component of redemption for the religious consciousness of Christians. Thus, although many incipient theories of his "atonement*" by death appear in the New Testament, Schleiermacher does not derive any theory of atonement from them. Essential for faith is the nature of the relationship between Christ and God. As the original*, ideal, complete, or perfect* human being in this respect, he is thereby rightly said to have a fully developed* God-consciousness* and to be wholly without sin. These are the qualities of Jesus' life that are passed on, albeit imperfectly, from generation to generation beginning with the community formed between Jesus the Redeemer and his original disciples, most notably the apostles he chose to accompany him. No miracle* is either desirable or required either to establish or to prove his unique connection with God—no virgin birth, no physical miracles, and no unnatural descent into hell, magical resurrection from death, or visible ascension into heaven. None of these views cast doubt, however, on the belief that as a natural human being chosen for his singular redemptive role by God and made conscious of this role by God, Jesus, beleaguered and tortured by his enemies, did die a horrible death and continued to live in communion with God after his death and that many of his immediate followers were together intensively conscious of his continuing presence among them by God's Spirit at that critical time. Apart from his self-proclamation* and teaching and, of course, the faithful memories and witnesses to his person and work thereafter, little more, if anything, is to be said about his life than this. The New Testament record offers no adequate ground for a biography of this human being other than these recognitions concerning his redemptive role. Although it might seem that he was sinless and perfectly conscious of God at each stage of his development as a person, how this did or could occur probably has to be kept open. The same is true of any theory that entails his reaching a point at which these qualities would have emerged. This second attempt, however, would be extremely difficult, perhaps impossible, to achieve since it has to face the reality of sin among those who interacted with him in his life and the consequent infection of their interpretation of his consciousness by sin.

Thus, in doctrine regarding Christ, two further aspects of Schleiermacher's view are to be highlighted. First, contrary to much traditional doctrine, Christ is not God, as such, and therefore has only a human nature, not a divine nature. However, he does have a completely formed God-consciousness, and this alongside his sinlessness is sufficient for redemption, the central purpose of his existence. Other things about him can be said, for example that he was a loving companion both to his disciples and to others he encountered. It may also be thought likely that certain things alluded to in the Gospel accounts actually happened. For example, given our current knowledge that large construction projects were proceeding in nearby Sephoris during his childhood and young adulthood, only six miles from Nazareth, and given that he was said to be a son of a carpenter, he might well have spent many of these years as a construction worker there and could not exercise his public ministry until his contract or forced labor was over. (This would be one of many attempts to explain what he did in those earlier years.) However, nothing about his life is of high significance except his redemptive activity. Second, that activity occurred inseparably through both the impression his person made and the actual work he did with people. One important aspect of that work is comprised in his self-proclamation that he is the Redeemer. Another important aspect lies in his proclaiming the reign* of God and demonstrating it in his life with people.

In *Christian Faith* the doctrines of regeneration* and sanctification* (CF §§106-12) represent the ongoing personal effects of Christ in the community of faith. I will rush through them at this juncture, for the essential points have already been registered and can be followed out further in the remaining sections of this chapter and in chapter 4. Those propositions are a nod to traditional doctrine, though as usual their contents are often freshly constructed. Under regeneration* are doctrines regarding "conversion*," the sudden or gradual beginnings of the new life in Christ, or "Christ in us," and "justification*," the continuing growth of that new life. Under "sanctification*" are doctrines regarding the "sins" and "good works" of the regenerate. The rest of part 2 consists successively of "the constitution of the world in relation to redemption," contained in doctrines of the church, and a culminating account of divine love and wisdom. All these doctrines begin with a dogmatic account of the church's "origins" in a pair of doctrines: "election" and "the communication of the Holy Spirit*."

Questions for Reflection

This carefully worked out position claims to be the likely best representation of what is given in the canon* of the New Testament, based on considerable devout and critical* investigation. To what extent does it seem plausible or perhaps convincing to you? What would you need to maintain a devout sense of relationship with God in Christ, and why?

Election and the Holy Spirit in the Church

Schleiermacher chooses to introduce all doctrine concerning the emergence of the church as a collective life of regenerated persons with one another through the two paired doctrines of election (*Erwählung*) and the Holy Spirit*. The election "of those who are justified is a divine predestination to blessedness* in Christ" (CF §19). In 1819 he published a lengthy essay critiquing the classic formulations on election by Augustine, by Calvin, and, in his own time, by the other most noted Reformed theologian in Germany, Carl Gottlieb Bretschneider (1776–1848). The results of this detailed examination of entanglements in their arguments he recapitulated in the two editions of *Christian Faith*. As an act "determined solely by the divine good pleasure" he cannot but see election as universal, as extending to an existence beyond death, and as expressed in "a single eternal divine decree*" founded in "the divine government* of the world" (CF §§117-20). That is to say, as an act of being made righteous by grace* through entrance into a life of faith, it is an event in the relationship of individuals in the community of faith, but there is no good reason to posit a double predestination. Eventually, all human beings are ordained to blessedness* in Christ. God loves all. In God's wisdom, and for all humanity, God arranges this.

Now have I got a surprise for you! Traditionally, the doctrine of the Holy Spirit has been framed in terms of the classical doctrine of the Trinity. As a result, theologians have had a hard time going on to this doctrine, usually identifying it mostly with inspiration of scripture and ecclesial authority. Thomas Aquinas, when he was trying to deal with it found himself struck dumb, lying prostrate before the altar, and gave up, having nothing more he could bring himself to say. I heard some of Karl Barth's relatively meager initial attempts at the doctrine in Basel, Switzerland. It seems as though he too had run out of things to say. In Schleiermacher's perspective, it is no wonder, for in his view to say "Christ in us" is the same as saying "the work of the Holy Spirit in the church and beyond." So, here is the surprise. In Schleiermacher's systematic presentation of doctrine, the propositions on the working of the Holy Spirit are by far the largest of all! Close examination shows that those doctrines are not restricted to §§121-25 on "the communication of the Holy Spirit" but explicitly run right through the entire doctrine of the church. There is so much that they cannot possibly be summarized with adequacy here.

What is special here is his understanding that the Holy Spirit is the shared, the "common spirit" (*Gemeingeist*) of the church. Think of the concepts "group spirit," "team spirit," and "public spirit" in ordinary language. Then expand this concept, as Schleiermacher and others sometimes did in their time, to "world spirit" (*Weltgeist*). Then take one more step and imagine that Spirit by which God continues God's activity of creation and preservation in the world, then God's activity for the purpose of redemption in that world in Christ, and then extend that activity to God's continuing presence in the world for that specific purpose. Consider all as an expansion of "the one eternal divine decree" in "the divine government of the world," in this case unfolding "the reign of God." That last mode or stage of God's activity is the "common spirit" of the church.

To be sure that he is not misunderstood, Schleiermacher uses two contrasting pairs of concepts: the fallibility versus infallibility of the church, continuing to latch upon his previous treatment of the sins versus good works of the regenerate as they are together sanctified (not divinized) and then the visible versus invisible characteristics of the church. The latter, it may be supposed, corresponds to the faithful's sense of God's revelation and God's hiddenness. It is not as though God withholds Godself from us. Rather, in our finite condition we are always unable to know God *in se*—in Godself—except by inference to know that God is love, which cannot be exactly defined in the finite, time-bound terms we have to use. God is not restricted to our attempts at forging stable categories either. God is always ahead of us, as it were. In biblical language, God's Spirit hovers over the waters. The wind of the Spirit blows where it will. When talking about the existence of the visible church as part of the world and alongside the rest of it, we can be quite specific. Schleiermacher pursues this task with the same open-ended, critical outlook that he has applied to every other theological task. *Christian Faith*, as the basic document on doctrine, has 172 propositions. Of those, at least 51 (§§113-63) are devoted specifically to this doctrine.[1]

Questions for Reflection

There can be no doubt that many of Schleiermacher's claims about election are contrary to much Reformation doctrine. Moreover, these claims are all couched in language consistent with his understanding of the Holy Spirit. Do you grasp the connection? Do you want nevertheless to hold that the Holy Spirit is (like) a separate person in the Godhead? If so, why? If not, why not?

The Shared Ministry of Clergy and Laity

A key element in Schleiermacher's doctrine of the Holy Spirit in the church is his view that all members of the church are called* to ministry*. The distinction between laity and ordained ministers of word and sacrament in the Evangelical church, he holds, is one of tasks, or functions, only. In his day, the clergy were among the few highly (university) educated persons. In the Reformed tradition to which he belonged, moreover, the tradition of an educated clergy was very strong, and it largely remains so. That tradition does recognize special ordinations to lay ruling elder and deacon, but generally there has been no other way to mark the special and distinctive gifts of laypersons or to provide intensive theological education opportunities for nonprofessionals apart from Sunday school and occasional meetings and retreats. In Schleiermacher's day any male could study theology at the university. Some individuals, moreover, could serve among leaders in the church, for which all theological study was intended in his view, but these were not required to have done theology. Consider *On Religion*, pages 3, 236, and 267-70, however. Those discussions allow for eventual gradations in the original distinction between clergy and "ordinary members."

In large part, the distinction persists to the extent that some persons must be charged with communicating, edifying, and quickening the whole community, whereas others are relatively "receptive" (*BO* §§278-79). "Care of souls" (*Seelenleitung, Seelsorge*) is especially exercised among the leadership for those who are lagging behind the rest in some respect, and this is the primary task to which practical* theology is addressed (*BO* §§263, 290, 300). Such is the case whether one is engaged in church service or church government. (See *BO* §§307-8, 315; also, under §334 see quotations of §§31-32 from the 1811 edition.)

It should be clear by now that, in a sense contrary to much Reformation doctrine, ministry (*Dienst*) is not equivalent to "ministry of word and sacraments." Nor, on the other hand, is it equivalent to "the priesthood of all believers," which would simply mean, as for the reformers, that all individuals have equal access to God and need no priestly mediator but Christ. However, he does place a very high value on preaching, within the general context of mutual witness by word and deed among all the faithful*. Even the preaching office, of which he mainly treats in the section on "Ministry of the Word of God" (*CF* §§133-35), is placed in the succession of Christ's proclamation* (*Verkündigung*), that of the apostles and the primitive church and that down the centuries to our own practice. Remember, this, too, is a part of the doctrine of the Holy

Spirit. Sometimes preachers report feeling especially "inspired," that is, in tune with the congregation and effective in "getting the message across." A major task of all the parts of theology, separately and in necessary conjunction, is to provide well-grounded criteria of judgment regarding these three claims.

In conclusion, try this key affirmation on for size: given the need for a critical treatment of all that is contained in scripture, it remains true that "everything must be traced back to the conception of Christ in scripture, in such a way that every individual may operate solely as an organ that brings scripture to mind and unfolds that content" (CF §133.1).

Questions for Reflection

Has this account of ministry shaken you at all? Do you agree with all of it? If so, why? If not, why not?

Revelation

In Schleiermacher's view, to the degree that any religion can be traced to an original "fact" or "starting point" and is not entirely explainable by what preceded it or by the present social context, that religion is based on revelation. This is the case no matter how much error may reside within it, for divine revelation is always associated with some human error no matter how much truth* it may possess. Revelation refers to the originating fact of a religion brought about by divine causality*, contained in the inspired communication* of some being or individual, and through the "impression" made by that being or individual registered in salvific "experience" by its "affective" noncognitive working. The impression works first and foremost on "self-consciousness." Moreover, revelation always comes within the context of a given society (a "positive" social configuration) and is never completely isolable from other social contexts associated with that society. Thus, all religion, of any kind and at any stage of religious development, is based on some revelation, on some divine communication* as just described. No religion, including Christianity, can establish the claim that it possesses the truth* pure and entire, for to do so would mean that God has made Godself known in it only as God is in Godself, and this is impossible given the limitations of human existence (CF §10 P.S.; cf. also §54.4). Now: "Conceived as divine revelation, the appearance of the Redeemer in history is neither something absolutely supernatural nor absolutely supra-rational" (CF §13; cf. also §92.4). That is to say, it is indeed supernatural but not as if the possibility for assimilating it did not already exist in human nature. Christ's existence, communication, and influence comprise a "natural fact," one that is drawn in part from Judaic religion contained in the Hebrew Bible and in subsequent expressions, and yet Christianity is not to be explained by that prior religion as if Christianity could have developed naturally out of it, that is, without the distinctively* new natural process that has taken place in Christ. Christ's appearance is also suprarational in that it is not rooted in, nor can its distinctive nature be encapsulated in, whatever reason anyone could have, and this is true of the entire compass of Christianity. However, what occurs in the Redeemer and redemption is also a "natural state" that would ideally receive the fullest possible recognition by reason that all human beings could share, to the point that the two could be indistinguishable and what the divine Spirit produces could be conceived as "the highest enhancement of human reason." All this does not mean, however, that Christian theology can be justifiably divided into a natural or rational theology on the one hand and a supernatural, suprarational "positive" theology on the other hand. This would not work, for there is no way to form "a systematic interconnection" between the two. With respect to their reference to inner experience, which could not be accessed by deduction or synthesis through generally recognized propositions, all genuine Christian doctrines are suprarational. With respect to their external expression, however, all these doctrines must be subject to the rules that regulate all rational discourse and in this way must be "entirely in accordance with reason" (CF §13; cf. also §§47.1 and 89.4).[2]

Questions for Reflection

Karl Barth and many others tend to hold that what separates Christianity from other religions is that its beliefs can be based on a final and exclusive "self-revelation" of God. Accordingly, in a proper sense other religions do not have authentic revelation at their base. Moreover, they could complain that Schleiermacher's view of revelation is either too subjective or too inclusive of what other religions might have, or (as Schleiermacher in fact claims) there could come a time when Christianity as we have known it could be superseded, or any combination of these characteristics could be superseded. Do any of these complaints bother you? If so, why? If not, would you be inclined to adopt Schleiermacher's position? (Remember, he wishes to claim that his position is likely the best representation of Evangelical faith.)

The Triune God

Schleiermacher struggled mightily with the seriously puzzling and inconsistent classical doctrine of the Trinity. In 1822 he published a lengthy historical-critical essay retracing the dialectical development of its formulations in the early centuries of the church, having laid out some of the difficulties and retrievable affirmations as the actual conclusion to the first edition of *Christian Faith* (1821–1822). In both places he set forth the system in a threefold form, closer to an imagined reconstruction of Sabellian doctrine (for which the original texts have not survived) than to the official Athanasian doctrine that had opposed it, thus without regarding God the Father, Christ, and the Holy Spirit as three separate and eternal persons or beings sharing certain attributes but not others. *Trinity** means "threeness." The official doctrine also affirms the oneness of the three as parts of God. Therein lies the basic problem; namely, how can there be a threeness and a oneness at the same time? The closest Schleiermacher could come to a satisfactory solution is this: God is indeed triune in God's fulfillment of the one eternal divine decree of redemption; but Christ was not preexistent, unless this simply means intended in the mind of God; Christ did not have two natures but possessed a perfect God-consciousness*; and Christ did not become God. The Holy Spirit, conceived as the common spirit* of the church, is the same thing as "Christ in us," the same thing as Christ's continuing presence in and through the church after Jesus'* death. In the second edition (1830–1831) he retained the same concluding account in a slightly rewritten form. (Ironically, the congregation

Schleiermacher served for nearly twenty-six years met in the *Dreifaltigkeitskirche*—the threefoldedness church; hence, I have taken the small liberty of calling it the Church of the Triune God.)

Questions for Reflection

It appears that a significantly large portion of those publishing systematic accounts of Christian doctrine today are purveying versions of the classic creedal* formulation of the Trinity. This number includes scholars who claim a "postmodern" orientation. The reason given lies in the postmodern assumption that all one can meaningfully give an account of is the particular social "world" to which one belongs, in this case that of the Christian church, and that in this world the creedal formulations are normative and cannot be doubted but can only be slightly improved upon at best. Now, since Schleiermacher's influence has spilled far beyond what the term *liberal* would even loosely describe, it has been easy not to use that label or the contrasting *conservative* label thus far. However, in this instance the contrast cannot be avoided. Schleiermacher's historical-critical handling of trinitarian doctrine is ostensibly liberal, even though he retains a positive account of the "triune" God. Moreover, he too holds with postmodernists that there exists no final, supreme, certain standard for appeal in controversial matters. However, he would reject the belief that church theologians have warrant to assume unquestionable authority for any traditional source, least of all those issued by those holding power at other periods of controversy from the fourth to the eighth centuries or that no other alternative could be authentically Christian. To do so is to make one's own formulations canonical, whereas even the canon of scripture is open. Do you see what is at issue here? Can you imagine how taking either of these approaches could well affect every other doctrine? Finally, what questions come to your mind concerning these two approaches?

Christian Ethics

With apologies, I have had to leave this great subject to the end. Moreover, I must present it in a form not nearly commensurate to Schleiermacher's own considerable but unfinished effort. I am truly sorry, for two reasons. First, despite numerous attempts to present this mammoth area of concern over the 170 years since Schleiermacher's death, the fruits tend to bear the very same difficulties that Schleiermacher said they would. In particular, they frequently display admixtures of rationalist and other philosophical teachings inappropriate for a distinctively Christian ethics, and those trends are so entrenched that it is very hard to sort them all out. Second, the few attempts to offer a truly "scientific" and "systematic" account in his terms seem to have proven equally inadequate, again despite some very powerful forays in that direction.

Schleiermacher himself made two extant efforts of this kind. The first, from 1822 to 1823 lies incomplete in the Jonas edition contained in SW I.12 (1843), a huge volume and a highly important one but so abstract and densely packed that it has not caught on. I know of two translations that are currently underway that might be attractive to some readers of English. The second, better-worked-out effort, from 1826 to 1827, is also from very detailed student transcripts, now being completed in a critical German edition by Hermann Peiter. I should obtain an English translation in the years ahead. From 1831 to 1832 Schleiermacher was trying to bring these into publishable form, but he got only as far as the introduction (1831).[3] Here I wish to offer a preliminary depiction of Schleiermacher's formal considerations and then to characterize what he was moving toward in specific content, to give you a taste. The formal requirements are quite clear, and I suspect you will find them significant. Briefly stated, they are as follows. (1) For Schleiermacher, Christian ethics is just as much faith-doctrine* as dogmatics* is. (2) Thus, great care must be taken to remove all traces of philosophical ethics from it, even if helpful parallels or complements may be recognizable there. That is, both dogmatics and Christian ethics refer to the same religious self-consciousness, God-consciousness (CF §61.3), and affective states. Both are grounded in an "immediate existential relationship" with God through Christ. If Christ is our prototype (*Vorbild*), our behavior must be patterned (*Abbild*) after him (CF §126.2). In that respect, the two subfields of dogmatics writ large are to be mutually corrective and, ideally, inseparable. In turn, their separation is not essential, but the subfield of Christian ethics is so little developed that it easily gets a scattered and overwhelmed quality when conjoined with dogmatics thus far (BO §223). (3) Christian ethics "will correspond far better to its relationship to faith-doctrine, consequently also to its own immediate determination, if it drops the imperative mood and simply describes how people live in the reign of God in all their relations" (CF §112.5). (4) To be avoided at all costs is the degeneration of its "rules for the Christian life" into "bare, [lifeless] prescriptions" (BO §224), whether because they are swamped by more developed dogmatic content or because they are presented separately. (5) In its systematic presentation a pure supernaturalist approach is also to be strictly avoided, for the same reasons that are applied to dogmatics (BO §224). (6) In doctrinal terms, our process of sanctification* in the Christian life is to be regarded as belonging to our participation in the reign of God, as are our temptations to sin (CF §§111.4 and 112). (7) In the reign of God everyone must show oneself to be "governed by Christ," in recognition of his "kingly power" (CF §105.2). By the same token, "all the personal influences" associated with Christ's "prophetic ministry" and "occurring separably in individual lives, often in part unintended and in part unsought, are the indeterminate and relatively fortuitous ministry" of all the community of faith, and that "belongs to Christian ethics" (CF §133.2). (8) Everything that depends on determining the point at which sin begins provides "much that is essential for Christian ethics" (CF §98.1). Correspondingly, all apparent divine penalties for all behavior are to be assigned to "the divinely ordained development of humankind" (CF §84.3). (9) "In the reign of God everything relates to everything else." Therefore, we cannot fail to share a common feeling (*Mitgefühl*, sympathy) with all those who are in misery, no matter what the state of our own blessedness may be, and to hope for the restoration (*Wiederherstellung*) of all human beings to a blessed relationship with God (CF Appendix to §163). (10) Finally, our efforts are hampered in that Evangelical ethics in its contrast to traditional Roman Catholic ethics has not yet been so fully worked out as in dogmatics (BO §225).

Although I have dubbed those ten requirements, pulled together from various passages in *Brief Outline* (1830) and *Christian Faith* (1830–1831), relatively "formal," they also point out some of the content of Christian ethics that we are to expect. An excellent summary of it is the Jonas edition of 1822–1823, which appears in Brian Gerrish's foreword to James M. Brandt's book *All Things New* (2001). Here I offer an even briefer further characterization of the forthcoming 1826–1827 Peiter edition, based on these requirements.[4] Bear in mind that Schleiermacher was putting the finishing touches on this work during the same period in which he was preparing the other two.

From here on, I largely follow the German theological ethicist Hermann Peiter, who has not simply confirmed my own investigations into Schleiermacher's Christian ethics but has also taught me a great deal.[5]

Reason, says Schleiermacher, cannot reproduce what the Spirit brings, but when it is a central and constant accompaniment of human existence, reason can become an instrument and organ of the Spirit*, which enables the church to arise and grow, thus to do what is good. In this sense, the divine Spirit never does without reason at any moment, but reason is never sufficient unto itself any more than is any other organ. Nothing essential can be transferred from philosophical into Christian ethics. For Schleiermacher "the proposition that all extra-Christian virtues are nothing but splendid vices can be carried out in all strictness," but in addition, unlike instruction in philosophical ethics, Christian ethics cannot possibly be exhausted in a theory of virtue. For example, at one point he lists four Christian virtues with respect to worship in the broader sense: purity, patience, forbearance, and humility. There are more. In any case, he said, if this subfield were to reach completeness, it would have to go through controversies over interpretation of scripture that had not yet arisen.

Nor can the theories of goods, virtues, and duties in philosophical ethics be paralleled in Christian ethics. *Virtue* by itself is not a Christian word, but *charisma* (gifts) is. Cultivation of "virtue" can certainly serve to strengthen a Christian's disposition (*Gesinnung*), but virtue is not that disposition. For an understanding of the latter, the source must be the New Testament. Yet, because current social conditions are different from those in New Testament times, New Testament content and current reflection must enrich each other.

For a Christian the chief aim is to grow in the Spirit, to be propagative, or generative, and thereby to be engaged in efficacious action. Thus, one wants more of what gifts the Spirit brings, notably love, and less of what gets in the way. That is, one's action is also "counteractive"; it is a "purifying," critical, reforming action. Sometimes what leads a Christian to action of either kind would seem irrational and absurd to ordinary practical reason. The reign of God is discovered when one finds an answer to the question, *where is the impossible possible?* This involves simple shared existence, celebration, and playing, in short, "joy* in God." This focus is not law; it is gospel. Thus, this kind of action proceeds from "the feeling of blessedness* itself," existence without concern (*Sorge*, worry) and without fear of life's vicissitudes, though one does want to offer care (*Pflege*) for what one has been called and eternally invited by God to share, notably through liturgy (*Cultus*) and worship in the broader sense that extends beyond worship services.

A third type of action, which Schleiermacher calls "presentational action," is the basis for community*, the growing of a possible society, not of an impossible one. Therein the church presents itself as a distinctive society, one, however, that does not know itself to be competent for each and every human being. That is, it is a community for piety* alone, and that within a given place and time. Only in this sense is Christian ethics a "positive" science (BO §§1 and 44), yet it is not simply something given, or posited, once and for all. In this sense, Christian ethics, viewed as a scientific discipline, emphatically does not fit neatly into an overall system of the sciences.

In Christian ethics experts offer information concerning health and disease in the Christian life. This work, therefore, not so much comprises a subject area as it is defined by the functions of service, or ministry*, such people perform in and on behalf of the church. In this way, it brings forth the "depth dimension" of reality represented by the mode of faith to be found there (BO §1). Like all the rest of theology—on which it depends—this discipline thereby exists to serve leadership* of the church based on people's relationship to God in Christ. Because it is guided by the divine Spirit, it is able preeminently to see love as something to be offered to others not because they are human beings in general but because they are specific persons in need of one's initiating that love before any receptivity is possible. This is so even if they are enemies (see Jesus' parable of the good Samaritan). Such love is a self-revelation of one's self as a Christian aiming at community. Thereby non-Christians become possible Christians. It is the same for them as for brothers and sisters in the faith. One gives that love simply in one's abiding, or resting, in God, for no other reason. It is at once a praising God and a giving out of one's self as a light unto the world. It is an efficacious action in which one's own initiative is a medium for God's own initiating love. Thus conceived, it is a spiritual act. Finally, it is not simply for one select kind of person to perform. Christianity is like a team sport, one in which all can have a part to play. Thus, here there is no contrast between clergy* and laity.

Now, to return to the beginning, we may ask: is Christian ethics supposed to be blind to what philosophical ethics sees? By no means! They both refer to the same matter at hand. However, Christian ethics looks with its own eyes at the world, just as the rest of theology does. This is not double vision, for the entire enterprise of reflective seeing presupposes* the Christian life in the first place. Its context for seeing, therefore, is that of the Christian life in the church and then in the rest of the world. Of itself, Christian ethics "cannot engender actions." Good works, as such, belong not to God's forum, then, but to that of the world (CF §112). That is to say, the matter at hand is profane, even when Jesus gives witness to it. Accordingly, while genuinely Christian ethics does not import philosophical ethics, it also does not foolishly refuse to acknowledge whatever matter at hand to which that ethics alerts it as the two kinds of ethics walk side by side.

Questions for Reflection

This account characterizes Schleiermacher's view of the form and content of the discipline of Christian ethics in contrast to the views he rejected. It is meant to be descriptive of generally Christian life from an Evangelical standpoint and not, as such, to bring about action, as if it possessed a ready-made set of prescriptions. Like all the other disciplines of theology, it is meant to encourage our own reflection on what to do and why. You might find yourself to be uneasy or to disagree with aspects of this view. If so, where and why? That is, where might you go to ground and test your own perspective on the Christian life?

CHAPTER FOUR

DEFINITIONS FROM SCHLEIERMACHER'S DISCOURSE

> *Definition . . . forms the transition between the concept formation and sentence formation. It is a major error to suppose that real definition and nominal definition are members of a kind, since only the real definition constructs an instance of knowing as an element of science, while the nominal [logical] definition constructs something arbitrary and fragmentary.*
> —*Dialectic, 47*

In effect, Schleiermacher's historical-critical arguments and conceptual analyses inaugurated a new, "modern" period in theology, in stark contrast to nonscientific, magical, supernaturalistic, rationalistic, suprarationalistic, and scholastic elements in medieval, Reformation, and post-Reformation theology. The following definitions of key concepts in his discourse may serve not only as material for readers to refer back to but also as summary characterizations of his thought. See the index for further delineations and uses.

Ideally, in a well-ordered, integrated "system" it should be possible approximately to access the whole of it through any part. Schleiermacher has such a system, in contrast to the "loci" lists of many previous theologians (for example, Philipp Melanchthon's *Loci theologici*). Thus, the rationale of the following alphabetical listing lies not only in affording ready access to the concepts themselves but also in getting at least a partial, tentative perspective on the whole as one proceeds. It also bears the advantage of allowing one to skip around at will.

Definitions are the shortest distance between ignorance and understanding. You may still need to labor a bit to keep all the components of each clearly in mind, but there is a wealth of ideas here to think about. I guarantee that doing the careful thinking required can handsomely repay your effort. This material is not old-fashioned, it is remarkably timely for doing theology today. I have interspersed some questions for reflection throughout these definitions to help you think through the issues raised by Schleiermacher's thought.

Anschauung: Perception*, intuition, gaining of perspective, vision (see ch. 2).

Apologetics: Not the usual defense, persuasion, or proof* of Christianity*, or a special form and/or party within it, nor a correlation of these with culture (Tillich); rather, as the externally oriented half of philosophical theology*, and strictly in service of church leadership*, its task is critically* to compare the distinctive* nature of Christianity and of any special form of it with that of other modes of faith*, thus, to secure its position among religious communities (see BO §§39, 43-53, 68; CF §§2, 11-14).

Art (*Kunst*): With some exceptions, until roughly Schleiermacher's time this term, though it was applied even to fine art, was almost exclusively restricted to the activity of craft—that is, work to achieve some preconceived end. His image was quite different. In his aesthetics lectures he also afforded room for free play and creative use of imagination, presenting an expression theory of fine art later borrowed by Benedetto Croce and further expanded by R. G. Collingwood and others. Outside fine art he tended to use the term in a "narrower sense" for "every ordered production whereby we are conscious of certain general rules whose application to particulars cannot be reduced to still other rules" (*BO* §132). Even in "scientific*" fields, however—and above all in philosophy* (cf. *Dialectic* 1811, §43)—following the rules is not enough; one must also unslavishly apply one's own sensibility, disposition, and skill; one must work it out for oneself, where possible also seeking general validity in what one produces. In this sense, he treats dialectic* as "the art of doing philosophy." Likewise, the activity of separating theological tasks from those of other fields—that of *Brief Outline*—he terms an "art" (*BO* §101). Accordingly, an ordered set of such rules that is derived only from "the nature of our entire procedure" he calls a *Kunstlehre* (theory of art, or technology). Hermeneutics* is such a theory, as is every part of practical* theology. This is why he insisted of his students that each one must work out one's theology for oneself.

Ascetic practice: This is roughly the same thing as devotional practice, but it is appropriately so only with certain reservations. Insofar as they correspond to the partial or temporary removal of sin* and the misery that results from sin, "moments of devotion [*Andacht*] contain an element of blessedness* only when they translate into thought or action, and ascetic practices include elements of blessedness only insofar as they are not actually ascetic, or at least not exclusively so, but are connected with vocational activity in some way or other" (*CF* §87.2; see Calling*). Thus, individual ascetic practices that are entirely divorced from the collective life of sin and grace are delusive and are not to be recommended.

Atonement: The closest Schleiermacher comes to a view of salvation through Christ's suffering and death is his account of Christ's reconciling (*versöhnende*) activity (*CF* §101), which is composed of Christ's taking up the faithful into "the community of his unclouded blessedness*." The inclusiveness he wishes to arrange for in his theology admits of a wide range of theories on this subject in the church as long as they do not seriously detract the faithful from this continuing reconciling activity. However, he takes the tendency of traditional views of Christ's work to involve either "magical* caricatures" or unrealistic expectations of people's gradual improvement through following Christ's example. The middle way between these extremes focuses on Christ's transformative influence before, during, and after his death. Hence in his writings and sermons references to a specifically saving event in his death are conspicuous by their absence.

Betrachtung: Typically, in his preaching Schleiermacher invited his listeners to join him in a *Betrachtung* (at once an observation, reflection, and meditation) on the words or events indicated in a biblical text. Accordingly, he tended to refer to his listeners as "devout" (*andächtige*) "friends" or "children" (of light). See Contemplation*, Proclamation*.

Bildung: See Culture*.

Blessedness (*Seligkeit*): This Hebrew word is baptized, as it were, for Christian use (cf. *CF* §91). For Schleiermacher it comes from participating in the perfect God-consciousness* of Christ; as such, it is a state of being, within the collective life of the regenerate*, that results from the redemption* accomplished by Jesus* of Nazareth. It is not a feeling. By grace*, the experience of regeneration* and sanctification* in Christ, through the common Spirit* of the church*, enables one's religious "sense and taste for the infinite* in the finite" (OR II) to rise to this state. Yet, in our contemplation* of God's presence with us we may find within ourselves an almost continuous sense of joy* (the major theme of *Christmas Eve*) and an accompanying disposition of gratitude in that state. This deep undertone of feeling is never far distant from "the tugging sadness and longing" (*Wehmuth**, cf. CF §120 P.S.; OR II n. 14 and V n. 14) that accompanies our imperfection, our need for redemption. In the reign of God* blessedness begins now and is never-ending; it is not deferred to an afterlife (CF §163; cf. Immortality*).

Calling, vocation (*Beruf*): One's calling as a Christian is summed up in one's will for the reign* of God; moreover, "nothing external to one's calling can be a good work" (CF §112.4). Even "genuine prayer* arises only when we engage in activities that serve to fulfill our Christian calling" (CF §147.2). That is to say, our calling to take part in "the collective life of blessedness" can never be purely ascetic; even one's devotional activities must issue in thought or action (§87.1). Special callings to ministry*, whether by clergy or laity (cf. BO §312) all obtain authenticity only under these conditions, not by virtue of any external rule or authority. While reviewing this chapter I heard of an African American pastor who had preached his last sermon one week before his death at 108. This pastor had notably fostered a call to ministry among his parishioners. His message was always "to keep the young within the hearing of God's call." Such a message was central within Schleiermacher's preaching and theology as well.[1]

Questions for Reflection

At this point, are you beginning to get a sense of what makes up Schleiermacher's own piety and approach to religious experience? Which elements belong, or do not belong, to your present approach and why?

Canon: The writings of the New Testament—the unique subject matter of exegetical* theology—are canonical "only insofar as they are held capable of contributing to the original, and therefore for all times normative, representation of Christianity*" (BO §103; cf. §§103-9). The canon's boundaries cannot be closed. Through the varying changes and developments of the Christian church this canon and the sacraments* together insure its "unity and identity" (CF §127; cf. §§128-32). Thus, in *Christian Faith* Schleiermacher's account of these scriptures is immediately followed by discussion on "the ministry of the Word*."

Care of souls (*Seelenleitung*): This activity is the defining feature of practical theology*, even when it refers to work within the structures of church government (*Kirchenregierung*). All theology, in fact, is done for the sake of church leadership (*Kirchenleitung*) viewed as qualified in this way. Although in Schleiermacher's time and place all these activities were carrried out by clergy*, his view on relations between clergy and laity and on the calling* and ministries* of the laity left the way open for a much less divided practice between the two. As it is every member's calling to witness, so it is everyone's calling to care for one another's needs.

Causality, divine: In Schleiermacher's view, for Christians the God revealed in Christ is "the living God," not a philosophical concept. However, in part 1 of *Christian Faith* he uses *causality* as an aid to defining divine eternity, omnipresence, and omnipotence in contrast to finite causality, with which it is not to be either identified or confused and is therefore termed "absolute" *(schlechthinnige)* (CF §§51-54). At the same time, he argues, this causality, "expressed in the feeling of absolute dependence, is completely presented in the totality of finite being, and in consequence everything for which there is a causality in God comes to be realized and does occur" (CF §54). This is tantamount to saying that God creates and preserves the world. With respect to redemption, in turn, tracing our restored communion with God to the divine causality indicated in part 2, "we posit the planting and spreading of the Christian church as an object of the divine government* of the world," and this divine causality herein "presents itself as divine wisdom and as divine love" (CF §§164-65).

Christ: This descriptor of Jesus' role and mission transfers the honorific Hebrew title "Messiah" into "Redeemer," Schleiermacher's usual ascription for Jesus' fulfillment of God's eternal decree* of redemption. Accordingly, "we [Christians] have communion with God only in a communion with the Redeemer in our lives. This communion is such that within it the Redeemer's absolute *[schlechthinnige]* perfection* and blessedness* exhibit a free activity proceeding from himself, but the need for redemption on the part of the recipient of grace exhibits a free receptivity by which we take grace into ourselves" (CF §91).

Christian religious immediate self-consciousness: In practice Schleiermacher tends to omit one or more elements of this phrase. In the doctrine of the church it tends to be reduced to one word: *consciousness.* Nevertheless, all these elements are always implicit, and, to be entirely precise, *Evangelical* should be added. Overridingly, this is a "consciousness of grace*," accomplished in and through Christ (CF §90), such that even consciousness of sin*, thus of our own need of redemption, is possible only by virtue of that grace. Thus, some version of this rubric is used throughout *Christian Faith* to represent not only the states of individual selves but also people's consciousness of divine attributes and of the way in which the world is constituted (the three "forms of dogmatic propositions" he features, CF §§30-31), either with respect (CF §29) to the contrast regarding redemption between grace and sin (part 2; see CF §§32-35) or as presupposed* by redemption (part 1; see CF §§62-63).

Frankly, every time I face this concept I have to reflect on it afresh. It is very complex, and yet, at base, it is also quite simple, for it all boils down to a fundamental feeling of piety*. Here is one way to unpack it: (1) our piety, to which all doctrine of faith* must directly refer, essentially consists in a relationship with God, viewed as the ultimate "whence" of our existence. (2) This relationship in piety, or faith, is a "modification of immediate self-consciousness" (CF §3.2), which each person experiences directly in a particular kind of feeling*—without any mediation or reduction to what we think or do, though both thinking and doing necessarily emerge from and express that feeling—and which each person also experiences receptively in accordance with one's own makeup and mode of acting (*eigentumliche Beshaffenheit und Handlungsweise*). (3) The "highest level" of self-consciousness is one in which one is able to feel absolutely (utterly, totally, unexceptionably) dependent in this relationship with God, yet "partially free" and therefore able to respond of oneself and not in a slavish dependency, but does not distinguish oneself from any other person or thing in this respect. That is, herein one tends to rise above both the state of other animals in whom feeling and perception confound each other and above the finite sensory/sensible (*sinnliche*) self-consciousness, which does rely on sense perception and on such comparisons or organic contrasts, though we are never able entirely to escape our embodiedness in the sensory domain (CF §§4-5). (4) This highest level of feeling is not identical to any other kind of feeling, though such affective states as contrition and joy; humility in recognition of all else that exists in God, humanity, and the rest of nature; and a soft satisfaction or pride in the light of spiritual gifts we have received emerge from that fundament. (5) Schleiermacher acknowledges that there are many ideas about how we get to this fundamental state of piety and other, derivative states. However, one particular account recommends itself to him among those that enjoy some currency* in the church; namely, one obtains one's own individual consciousness of grace first through some manner of participation in the collective life, especially the "common spirit" (Holy Spirit*) of the community of faith (the church*); our own subsequent unmediated Christian self-consciousness emerges from that experience. "The new life of each individual springs from that of the community, while the life of the community springs from no other individual life than that of the Redeemer" (CF §113.1).

Christianity (*Christentum*): This term has both a mostly normative and a mostly descriptive meaning. The first meaning refers to the genuinely grounded faith of the regenerate* and the community* of faith they represent—"one," "infallible" and "invisible," as it were (CF §§148-49). The second meaning refers to the divided, fallible, and visible church, which moves toward its "consummation*." Another term, *Christendom (Christenheit)*, refers to a sociopolitical culture in which the church is or was historically predominant. Schleiermacher sometimes referred to the German states as constituting a (nominally) "Christian" country or society, but he did not employ either term for this purpose.

Church: In a broader sense, *church* is equivalent to "religious community*" and is an ethical, sociological term. In a narrower sense, it is the "Christian" or "Evangelical" community of faith but with the provisos mentioned in the previous item. "Evangelical church" mainly contrasts with "Roman Catholic church." As composed of Lutheran and Reformed descendants of the magisterial Reformation, it also contrasts with smaller churches that descended from what was later called the "radical" or "left-wing" Reformation.

Clergy: Those specially ordained to ministry*. See chapter 3.

Communication (*Mitteilung*): In addition to the usual meanings, Schleiermacher holds that Christ's sinless perfection* and blessedness* are "communicated" to the faithful*. To translate this term as "imparted" would be misleading in this respect because it would suggest infused, pipeline action from a distance (as in gracious divine action typically associated with Augustinian doctrine).

Community, Communion (*Gemeinschaft*): As in John Dewey's work, notably *Individualism Old and New*,[2] Schleiermacher viewed community and individual as existing in a reciprocal relation, and he did so on the same empirical* and moral* grounds.

Individuals* are to be respected, and their fundamental human rights are to be accorded in community. They are to be correspondingly responsible in community. Children are to be educated* for these purposes. Faithful Christians share *Gemeinschaft* with Christ. Note: John Dewey (1859–1952), who held similar views, was born only twenty-four years after Schleiermacher's death. It is known that he early had to come to terms with, then largely to reject, Hegel's style of thought, but it is not yet known whether he drew from Schleiermacher.

Confessions: see Creeds*.

Consciousness (*Bewusstsein*): This is an individual's state of discerning awareness of some "other," notably in Schleiermacher's usage, of God or of the genus humanity, also of or from oneself. Religious and especially Christian* "self-consciousness" is not *of* oneself (in which oneself would be the one addressed) but *from* oneself toward God in relationship (treating God, however, as subject in that relationship, not as a mere object). One can, of course, also be conscious of an event or action or of some kind of concept or whole of anything, for example, of grace* or the world*. See Christian* self-consciousness, species-consciousness*, God-consciousness*.

Questions for Reflection

Even by some Protestants, Schleiermacher has often been accused of being overly (negatively) critical of Christian tradition and of being "subjective." Thus far, do you detect some possible reasons for these criticisms and some responses Schleiermacher would make? Where do you (tentatively) stand and why?

Consummation (*Vollendung*): Consummation points to the possible final states of the Christian church and of individuals, topics not for regular faith-doctrine* but for prophetic* doctrine only (CF §§157-63; see also OR V).

Contemplation (*Contemplation*): This word refers to meditative reflection. On rare occasions it is a near synonym for *Betrachtung** within Christian community. Schleiermacher tended to think of people of faith* as called* to and capable of such reflection, thus it is a primary evocation (vs. rule-giving) in his Christian ethics* and sense of worship as well. See Reflection*.

Contrasts (*Gegensätze*): In his dialectical* sense, according to which ways that concepts work, or what can be conceived of within organic* conditions, lead to the result that contrasts are never pure opposites. This is so, for two or more contrasts always bear some characteristics of what they are distinguished from, though in varying degrees. It is important to show how they are different from each other. Schleiermacher frames much of his conceptual world in such terms, which are more qualitative or value*-related than quantitative in nature.

Conversion: The first of two propositions regarding "regeneration*" defines *conversion* as follows: "In each individual, conversion, viewed as the beginning of the new life in communion with Christ, is manifested through repentance, which consists of the combining of regret and change of heart, and through faith*, which consists of a person's taking the perfection* and blessedness* of Christ* into oneself" (CF §108). Carefully pieced together out of Evangelical* confessions* and in accordance with "general devotional practice" among the Evangelical churches, this doctrinal definition stands among those that most clearly ward off the mode of faith* in those churches from that of the Roman Catholic Church. *Conversion* points to an aspect of faith experience that gradually unfolds. No one order or pattern of it bears precedence over the others. As an aspect of regeneration, one sustained over time, justification* is the other element of faith experience paired with conversion. The two are "symmetrical"; they occur "at the same time." Issues regarding proclamation* of the Word*, communion* with Christ, preparatory grace*, and baptism are deeply embedded in a proper understanding of this doctrine.

Creeds and Confessions: These are formal documents by which churches have distinguished their respective sets of beliefs from one another. Like most other theologians, Schleiermacher tends to use the term *Symbolum* (symbol) for ancient creeds, reserving *Bekenntnisschriften* (confessional writings) for more elaborate, territorially identifiable statements of belief (French, Hungarian, and so on). He is a staunch critic of such documents wherever he finds assertions or anathemas that serve more to divide than to unite churches. Frequently, however, in presenting faith-doctrine* he features examples of both tendencies, using critical comparison of them as one ingredient in his construction of doctrine for the Evangelical* churches in Germany, viewed as one church. In this light, he views doctrines that do no harm to popular piety* as tolerable though not acceptable for dogmatic* purposes.

Criticism, critique (Kritik), critical (kritische): Like hermeneutics*—a discipline with which it is dialectically* paired—historically, *criticism* is (1) primarily a term of general usage regarding the study of texts: "philological criticism." Thus, in its basic rules it is not restricted to, or in the service of, any special interest such as biblical study. In this primary usage, it can be divided into "higher" and "lower" criticism, though in most respects their actual methods are indistinguishable. The greatest task of higher criticism is to establish the canon* (BO §110) based on both internal and external evidence. The most distinctive task of lower criticism, which determines the predominant meaning of criticism in Schleiermacher's early life, is "to separate out the original reading as accurately and convincingly as possible" (BO §118) and the history of the text (BO §120). By extension, when Schleiermacher prepared his *Critique* of previous ethical theories (1803), he aimed simply to set the record straight on the meanings of those theories in comparison with each other. He waited to display his own theory until the three-year period that followed. (2) Schleiermacher helped establish a second, closely allied sense, carried in the expression *historical-critical method*. This method applies the same general and careful attention to historical matters, now not neglecting to fix upon relatively stable, changing, and developing contexts within which those matters reside. Such historically oriented criticism he pursued in interpreting ideas, arguments, and processes at once in exegetical* theology; in church history and history of doctrine; and in dogmatics*, Christian ethics*, and church statistics*. (3) Philosophical criticism was represented in a big way in Kant's systematic "critical" work, notably in his three *Critiques* of pure reason, practical reason, and judgment (1781–1804). More broadly in Schleiermacher's practice, even this critical philosophy was to be thoroughly critiqued. Here, the elements of analyzing the form and content of thinking logically (for impropriety, inconsistency, and comparative inadequacy—part of "dialectic" in his usage), empirically (for sufficient grounding in reality) and regarding untenable presuppositions (for example, of a transcendental sort) were added in, along with a then barely developed "heuristic" feature that had to do with raising appropriately formal questions and examining ill-formed questions (also part of his dialectic). Schleiermacher's use of all three types of criticism became standard in his systematic*, scientific* work, evident in all his writing and lecturing in the thirty years after 1804. Closely interconnected with his hermeneutical method, these tools enabled all of his sizeable contributions to modern thought. (4) In this light, I have termed his distinctive philosophical approach to science and other scholarship *critical realism*, this in contrast to the dominant trends of idealism associated with Fichte, Schelling, and Hegel for which his period has been mistakenly best known until quite recently.

Culture (Bildung): That which is highly developed, educationally speaking. Otherwise it is an unsettled term in Schleiermacher's usage, a product of an age in which very few people had gotten very far in school, though it suggests advanced normative qualities that are to be fostered publicly. *Kultur* is employed for other, more descriptive uses, as in French (high) culture. As an adjective *gebildete* refers to the more educated classes or, more normatively, to those whose practice is more intellectually, aesthetically, and/or morally refined. See also Education* and Development*.

Currency, having (geltend): Ordinarily, in Schleiermacher's theological usage "to have currency" bears much more the connotation of being an authentic representation of faith and thus of being reputably current than the stricter connotation of "to have validity." This slant reflects his markedly historical, pragmatic* orientation to matters of meaning and truth*. For example, cf. *Brief Outline* §97, also *Christian Faith* §19, which states: "Dogmatic* theology is the science* concerned with the interconnection* of doctrines that have currency in a given social organization called a Christian church* at a given time." On the other hand, in order to have "currency" such doctrines must have both "warranty" (CF §27) and "exactitude" (CF §16). It is neither necessary nor sufficient that they enjoy "prominence" (CF §25) or that they be generally regarded as "orthodox*" (CF §25 P.S. and BO §§203-11; cf. CF §131.2).

Decree, the one eternal divine: There being no ground for separating aspects of God or God's will from God's act, as many have tried to do, the divine decree of redemption in Christ is itself one with the divine government* of the world and is eternally so. (See Schleiermacher's arguments in CF §§90.2, 109.3, 117.4, 120.4 and 164.2.)

Deity (Gottheit): Schleiermacher often uses this term as a general receptacle for any reference to divine attributes. At the same time, he uses it to obviate any suggestion that God is a singular being or person after the pattern of human beings. Of course, the quality of God in relationship is both "personal" and "person-forming," preeminently in relation to Christ* and then in relation to all other human beings, just as God relates to all the other aspects of the creation in ways appropriate to them.

Dependence, the feeling of absolute (das schlechthinnige Abhängigkeitsgefühl): Although this concept appears very frequently in *Christian Faith* after being introduced in §4 (§9 in the first edition), it is among the most widely misunderstood. It has the same meaning in both editions, used as a kind of litmus test for a theological understanding of the experience of Christian faith*. In both propositions the doctrinal statement itself says that "the nature of Christian piety*" consists in the fact that "we feel ourselves to be absolutely [*schlechthin*] dependent," which means the same thing as saying that we are "conscious" that our existence utterly, purely, unexceptionably occurs "in relation to God." By God he especially means "the Supreme* Being." This, he states, is "the highest stage" of religious feeling*. Even in monotheistic religions, wherever an element of mere "theophany" (visible manifestation of God or of a god) is present, that feeling is not absolute, not pure, or unadmixed with feelings that do not belong to it. Thus, it is not meant to be a description of religious experience in general or throughout history. Christ has brought to us the relationship with God to which alone *Christian Faith* intends to provide a systematic account. Finally, when Schleiermacher uses the short form indicated in his discussion of §4 in 1830, he notes his pleasure—at a time when many scholars were seeking appropriate forms to render latinate words in German—in finding the adjectival form *schlechthinnige* in place of the adverbial form *schlechthin* for the purpose. That is all. The word means "absolute," though it is sometimes helpful to use other words to explain it, as Schleiermacher himself has done. See Piety*.

Development *(Entwicklung)*: Since Jean-Jacques Rousseau (1712–1778) had introduced the notion that human beings go through stages of development, Immanuel Kant and a few other thinkers of Schleiermacher's time had begun to make some mostly rather vague use of it, and Schleiermacher did too, notably in his *Soliloquies* (1800) and in his lectures on education*. For him it chiefly means literally an "unfolding" of potentials, usually in "stages" variously described depending on the subject matter. Sometimes he depicts the development of a person or of some feature of life such as religion as the unfolding of a distinctive "idea" or enabling principle, or as the unfolding of inherent purpose. He deems Christian faith and the history of it to be "teleological*" in this sense. There is no concretely predictable end to this process.

Dialectic: (1) When taken from the triad physics, ethics (the human sciences), and dialectic, developed especially by Plato along with other ancient Greek thinkers, *dialectic* means the proper way to think about relations of knowing to being in either of the other two domains of inquiry, that is, "the art of philosophizing." The concept also refers to any such activity in and among the "sciences*," which were not much separated from philosophy until the Renaissance. (2) In addition, the word refers to a type of relation between concepts—usually but not necessarily in pairs—in such a way that they are to be defined in terms of each other, sometimes even to the point of being so interdependent as to be virtually "identical*" in some specified sense. Schleiermacher's discourse very often moves in this way. (3) As suggesting a quality of "conversation," Schleiermacher's practice of dialectic is fundamentally "dialogical," in the Christian sense seeking always to be "speaking the truth in love,"[3] in openness and respect, and in expectation of learning from the other person.

Discourse *(Rede)*: Among the several modes of discourse Schleiermacher uses, "rhetorical" is perhaps the most prominently qualified and restricted in his definition of it, for in his view (as for Plato) rhetorical traditions had tended fully to dominate schooling and public discussion since the time of Socrates, along a path antithetical to philosophy. That is, the tendency was to treat reality as contained, undynamically and noninteractively, in neat little boxes, and accordingly to form language in like containers, forcing decisions to go strictly one way or some other predetermined contrasting way, and language was used preeminently to exposit or persuade. Historical-critical thinking and allied disciplines represent Schleiermacher's preferred alternative to these traditions. These traditions, despite the astonishingly rapid development of philosophy and the sciences over the past two centuries, are still quite dominant in schooling and public discourse today. Now, the *Reden* delivered *On Religion* are discourses that combine rhapsodic personal expression with rhetorical efforts to awaken historical-critical thinking more than to exposit or persuade and with an aim to awaken philosophical-scientific understanding. His sermons over the years are discourses in which the rhapsodic feature has dropped out almost entirely and rhetorical, didactic (teaching), and dialectical* (CF §28) elements combine. The effort there is to beckon listeners thoughtfully to contemplate* their own faith* and that of the Christian community* that surrounds them. Neither type of discourse employs the more purely didactic-presentational language he found necessary in order to express thinking about the subject matter of theology "scientifically*." None of these discourses, moreover, are "speeches" in the sense for which we would ordinarily use the word. (The great early-twentieth-century English religious philosopher John Oman could think of them in that way, but I doubt that we can reasonably do so.) Each discourse is addressed to an audience, to be sure, but not at all in the spirit of earlier dominant rhetorical traditions. Rather, they are invitations to shared thought and reflection. Even though they are quite popular in style, they mirror more of a philosophical and scientific bent of mind. They are meant to stimulate conversation and are thus delivered in the spirit of dialogue.

Distinctiveness (*Eigentümlichkeit*): This term indicates a set of qualities or behaviors that express what is special about an individual entity as compared with some more general set of categories or descriptions. As an historically-critically minded thinker Schleiermacher always placed such qualities of self or social entity in a larger context. He always did so, however, in order to be able to sort out what might be distinctive about each one within those communities, circumstances or relationships with others. Accordingly, the terms *individual* and *community* are always dialectically* related in his discourse.

Questions for Reflection

Since the last issue's paragraph, are you beginning to grasp some major elements of Schleiermacher's theological style and approach? In particular, can you now use his understanding of conversion as an example? Are you able to adopt these elements as your own? If so, why? If not, why not?

Divine (*göttliche*): Of or pertaining to some conception of or claimed activity of God—not necessarily of God thought of on the analogy of a human person. See Deity*, God-consciousness*, Supreme* Being; cf. *God* in chapter 3.

Dogmatic theology, dogmatics (*Dogmatik*): The dialectical* and systematic* study and resultant knowledge, by those who hold Christian conviction, that now has currency in the Evangelical Church or other Christian church (BO §§195-96 and cf. §§197-231; CF §19 and cf. §§15-18). Schleiermacher indicates that any other part of the "social condition" of the church could also be a special subject area but that none other had been developed at that time. In principle, Christian ethics (cf. ch. 3) would be a coordinate aspect of dogmatics, but it was not yet possible to achieve this kind of conjoined treatment as yet. Moreover, because dogmatics arises out of the church (though total agreement there is not necessary), he recognizes no status for individual dogmatics. His actual discussion of the definition and method of dogmatics in the introduction to *Christian Faith* (§§1-31) is very detailed and therefore cannot be adequately covered in the present book. Especially among the Evangelical churches, *dogmatics* is a traditional term for a more systematic*, cohesive, and scientific* presentation of Christian doctrine, not in the more pejorative sense of hidebound "dogma" but in the sense of a teaching that has currency* in the church, in this case specifically and distinctively* the Evangelical (Lutheran and Reformed) churches in Germany in Schleiermacher's time (see especially *CF* §§1-2, 10-15, 19, 27-28).

Education *(Erziehung)*: The same word is used for child-rearing and for learning of the young in schools or through tutoring. Next to Johann Heinrich Pestalozzi (1746–1827), but with a reputation for more systematic thinking, in this field Schleiermacher is best known among early modern educational theorists for his progressive, developmentally* oriented views of these processes and for similarly liberal views on higher education.

Empirical thinking: In Schleiermacher's usage there are two distinct meanings: (1) chiefly, it is an attention to spacial-temporal particulars in nature*, including human experience. This element must always be present in thinking that purports to be scientific* and that intends to fulfill the aims of either description or explanation, and it must be interactively accompanied by speculation* (or rational process). (2) In theology the "empirical" can represent a tendency to restrict understanding of doctrinal matters—notably regarding Christ and the essential elements of the Christian church—to natural phenomena, thereby excluding reference to anything supernatural*. In Christology this tendency is associated with Manichean heresy and in doctrine regarding salvation and the Christian life with Pelagianism. The main consequence of this approach is a deluded view, namely that Christ exercises influence by means of example alone and that recipients can climb from the collective life of sin toward increasing perfection only by this means (see especially *CF* §§100.3 and 101.3-4).

Ethics: In Schleiermacher's usage this English word points to several distinguishable meanings in German. (1) *Ethik*: His 1804–1806 "notes on ethics" (Wallhauser and Tice 2003) and subsequent notes for lectures in philosophical ethics refer to theoretical, philosophical, and methodological study of the entire human domain, which Wilhelm Dilthey (1833–1911), following his lead, called the *Geisteswissenschaften* or "human sciences." Actually, he takes every other science, including what Dilthey called the *Naturwissenschaften* but also mathematics and various technical and auxiliary studies, to contain some elements of ethical concern in them at various levels of human interaction and conduct—the personal, the interpersonal, the social, the communal and commercial, and the political (the state and how society at large is organized and led). (2) Covering the same ground but comprising a narrower set of interests is philosophical *Ethik*, or *Sittenlehre*, which focuses on principles of conduct (*Handlung*) or morals and customs (*Sitte*, a word used for both of the latter), or "the principles of history." This field is divided into introductory matters, then theories of "the highest good," "virtue," and "duty." (3) *Christliche Sittenlehre*, or *Ethik*, had not hitherto received the same sort of concentrated, systematic inquiry as could be found in dogmatics*, so he organizes the subject quite differently, referring to the distinctively Christian "life" (*Leben*; cf. ch. 3). (4) Morality (*Sittlichkeit*) refers to various organizations and principles of moral life studied in all those fields of inquiry.

Evangelical: See Dogmatics*; see also chapters 2 and 3. When capitalized here, Evangelical Church refers to the mainline Protestant institutional church in Schleiermacher's own time and place.

Evil (*Übel*): Schleiermacher's very complex critical analysis of views about evil and its relation to Christian faith and life cannot be readily summarized. In the end, however, his position reaches a high-water mark among discussions of the subject. The philosopher-theologian John Hick has argued that he offers the best formulation of an answer to the problem that the God of love permits evil.[4] The key to Schleiermacher's position is God's ordaining human freedom*, which has issued in a condition for the arising of social and individual evil (*Böse*; cf. CF §84.2). Further, both natural and human evil, he holds, are ordained by God, but there is no total separation and independence of evil from good (CF §§48-49). Moreover, although some sin brings about some natural evil, there is no "magical*" connecting of sin and natural evil (CF §§75-78). Nor does it make sense to posit a golden age when evil did not exist (CF §§59-60). Christ's sinlessness, however, serves as an enablement for seeing that human evil can be overcome and for experiencing redemption* from such evil (CF §§93-94; cf. §101.3). In this connection, the "unstable" idea of the devil has no significant scriptural warrant and lies astride the boundaries of faith-doctrine* (CF §§44-45; cf. §72.2).

Exegetical: See Historical* theology. This discipline focuses on the documents and contexts of the early church (primitive Christianity).

Faith (*Glaube*): For Schleiermacher, almost everywhere in his writing, this term, which in ordinary German usage can refer either to belief or faith, means faith, or religious experience (cf. ch. 2), that is, what is immediately present in or directly rooted in Christian "religious self-consciousness*." In contrast, belief is a cognitive (*erkennende*) activity, issuing in opinion and information or supporting facts or knowledge (*Erkenntnis*). See Knowing*, also *Christian Faith* §3.4, where the feeling state to which *faith* refers is taken to include "conviction" as an aspect of "piety*."

Faith-doctrine (*doctrina fidei, Glaubenslehre*): This theoretically inseparable counterpart to Christian ethics* or "morals" (*Sittenlehre*, BO §§223-25, 229) treats "the basic fact" of faith* as "something original" for historical theology of all kinds (BO §80).[5]

Faithful, the (*Gläubigen*): These people may also be believers in certain sets of beliefs, but in Schleiermacher's usage a *Gläubige(r)* is almost always thought of as a person of faith*, and *die Gläubigen* are the faithful, faithful persons, not "believers" as such.

Feeling (*Gefühl*): See chapter 2 for an analysis of this term.

Free spiritual power (*freie geistige Macht*): Here *geistige* very much includes use of intellect. Even "the construction of a fact, the combination of outer and inner* into one historical perspective [*Anschauung**], is to be regarded as a free action of the mind" (BO §152). Here the reference is especially to a free "discretionary" influence in church government versus "binding" authority formed in a previous epoch. This is an influence practiced in a "discretionary" manner upon the whole by a person who feels "called*" to do so (BO §§312-14, also 328-34). These persons prominently include writers and "academic teachers." Such power alone "can initiate reforms" (§314; cf. also Schleiermacher's powerfully insightful interpretation of the Reformation in the 1817 *Oratio*, Nicol 2004).

Free will versus determinism: In a series of writings over the years, Schleiermacher worked out a philosophical examination of the inherently contestable problem of free will in relation to a world order determined by God. One set of options that he thereby rejected would be to hold either one of these two views to the exclusion of the other, even though ample evidence exists to support both. Another option, which it is arguable he came to, is to show that the two views are compatible. In recent decades many philosophers have tried out this option. To my mind, however, this solution presents sufficient difficulties so as not to be sustainable either, and I am not convinced that he thought it could be. Another possibility, which he appears to have entertained, is to accept the two views as permanently in tension, as apparently paradoxical given our present capacity to understand. If one considers the way he treated a closely allied problem, that of free will and absolute dependence, this resolution seems plausible. That is, in *Christian Faith* (§4) he argued that human beings are indeed absolutely dependent but are also "partially free." God created us in such a way that we could exercise free will but always only under the condition that we could not transcend the natural order (however changing that might be) that God has ordained and continually preserves. This combination of the two views is essential for his proposed solution to the problem of evil*.

Freedom: See under Dependence* and Evil* and Free* will.

Questions for Reflection

How might we learn to live with this seeming paradox? Suppose you were a teacher or psychotherapist. When or to the extent that you begin to see some possibility of insight or real change in behavior in the person you are working with, your tactics of support and encouragement can be directed to the person's capacity for free will. When or to the extent that you see how greatly in bondage to patterns of self or circumstance the person is, you could empathetically, patiently, and understandingly emphasize the debilitating consequences of being caught in a net of determinism. Combining the two kinds of tactics can help bring change and healing. This is how Schleiermacher operated in every part of his life. You do not have to decide whether free will is absolutely available or whether the deterministic systems that impinge on human life can be somehow broken through. You simply act as if both were true and lovingly watch for positive consequences. Does this approach strike you as pro or con?

Gefühl: See *feeling* in chapter 2.

God: See chapter 3, also Deity*, Divine*, Supreme* Being.

God-consciousness (*Gottesbewusstsein*): For Christians*, that one Other to which our higher, immediate self-consciousness refers in the feeling of absolute dependence* of ourselves and all else is termed *God*. Therein the inseparable consciousness of God is the same as being in relation to God (CF §4). Everything else we can properly say about God is a correlate of this feeling and relationship. God-consciousness assumes no prior knowledge of God. Furthermore, God is no mere external object of sensory self-consciousness, nor is God-consciousness necessarily joined with any such lower consciousness. Rather, our God-consciousness is absolute, unchanging, and self-identical throughout. In dogmatics*, along with experience of divinely caused* redemption* accomplished through Jesus*, it is the fundamental criterion by which the authenticity of every doctrine of faith* is to be measured. Further, for Christians the perfected, sinless quality of God-consciousness in Jesus is what is especially communicated* through his proclamation* of himself and of the reign* of God to the regenerate* in the founding and continuation of the church*. It is a consciousness that arises in relationship with God, who is present to the faithful* in Christ* (Jesus as the Redeemer*) and in the common spirit of the church (the Holy Spirit*). Wherever there exists a presentiment* of this full consciousness of God, it is an activity of preparatory* grace. In every moment of Christian faith and life, however, God-consciousness and relationship to Christ take place only in combination. Thus, in the Christian domain there can be no natural theology* related to consciousness of God alone apart from redemption* and no theology of Christ apart from God-consciousness (CF §62.3). This inseparably twofold communion and action is called grace* (CF §64). Therein we participate in a collective state of grace and a collective state of sin, the latter of which inevitably remains in part as it is gradually disappearing (CF §§86-87, 106-7).

Government of the world, divine (*göttliche Weltregierung*): This large-scale activity of God plays an essential, indivisible role in the entire Christian story. That is to say, the reign* of God, or the planting and extension of the Christian church, is its object (CF §§164-65; cf. §114.2). In accordance with this divine government, however, Christ's so-called kingly office is purely spiritual, and it does not appear prior to the growing activity of grace* through him in the community of faith* (CF §105.1).

Grace: From the Christian standpoint that Schleiermacher upholds, grace is that continuation of God's creative-preserving activity which becomes a person-forming activity by virtue of the being of God in Christ, through whom members of the community of faith, efficaciously affected by him, approximate to blessedness*. Thus, the God-consciousness* accomplished in grace through Jesus the Redeemer* is to be considered "the completion of the creation of human nature"; Christ may be described as "the second Adam"; and sin* is to be seen as "ordained" by God's "decree*" for this purpose. Grace is received and assented to by faith (CF §§86-91).

Hermeneutics: The general art of getting an accurate, authentic interpretation of discourse* of any kind, written or spoken. In addition to introductory matter, it is comprised of two parts: the "grammatical" part, which investigates an author's use of what is available through the styles and structures used in a given language tradition (for example, in German) and the "technical" or "psychological" part, which investigates the author's own distinctive* language and thought. All that the exegetical* study of the Scriptures adds to this general art are certain "auxiliary" studies and techniques necessary to perform these two interlocking tasks in ways appropriate to the various languages, historical backgrounds, and genres to be found in these writings. Thus, contrary to what had long been thought, there is no hermeneutics special to them. Hermeneutics is inextricably intertwined with philological criticism*. Schleiermacher is the undisputed founder of modern hermeneutics, though discovery of his key role is still underway today.

Historical theology: This set of disciplines "attempts to exhibit every point of time in its true relation to the idea of 'Christianity.' " As such, it constitutes "the foundation of practical theology*" and the "verification of philosophical theology*" (BO §27). The community of faith it studies is thereby regarded as "a historical entity" that is to be understood both in its "present condition" and, in each case, as "a product of the past" (BO §26). It also resides at "the inner core" of "the modern study of history," that is, in "the [general study] of ethics and culture" (BO §69), and within it any other historical treatment of its "facts" are "strictly subservient" to it, though the basic principles of historical study are the same for both (BO §70; cf. CF §19). Further, because the "basic fact of" Christianity is firmly established as "something original," the only study of it can be that of its "development*" (BO §80). Historical theology has three divisions: the study of primitive Christianity, of its total career, and of its present state, hence the divisions of (1) exegetical theology*, (2) church history and the history of dogma and of Christian ethics (cf. BO §183), and (3) church statistics* and both dogmatic* theology and Christian ethics*.

Identity (*Identität*): In Schleiermacher's discourse this term represents a very important multilayered set of relational concepts borrowed from his notes and lectures on *Dialectic**. See my 1996 translation of the 1811 *Dialectic* notes, the detailed index there, and my discussion of six types in "What Does 'Identity' Mean?" within the introduction, xvii-xviii. Usually the context tells one which meaning he intends.

Immortality: Schleiermacher finds no general, philosophical arguments for life after death to be feasible. In any case, they would not be pertinent to Christian doctrine. In fact, after careful examination of various purported indications and proofs, Schleiermacher finds no strong grounds in the experience of Christian faith or in the picture of the Redeemer (CF §§98.1, 158.1-2) to assert anything definite about the survival of personal* existence after death. The closest thing to such an affirmation would be to say that if Christ so survived then all human beings would survive (CF §§158.2, 163 P.S.). At best, allied biblical expectations fall under the rubric of "prophetic doctrine" (CF §§159-63), because we can have no experience of it. Both the imagined vision of the church's consummation and that of personal survival, whether taken singly or together, present us with such difficulties that we can never attain to a well-defined, perspicuous view of either one (CF §163 P.S.). See Election in chapter 3.

Incarnation (*Menschwerdung*): At most, Schleiermacher makes only rare, incidental use of this term, for it suggests a preexistent Christ. Instead, the idea that "the Word became flesh and dwelt among us . . . we have beheld his glory" (John 1:14) became the motto for *Christmas Eve* and for his entire system of doctrine. In the introduction to *On Religion* V, he uses this image as a metaphor for the presence of religion in the various religions. In *Christian Faith* the guiding principle is that "the activity of the Redeemer* proceeds from the being of God in him"; thus, it is "a continuation of that same person-forming divine influence on human nature" (CF §100.3). The influence of Christ*, in turn, "consists solely in the human communication* of the Word*, but only insofar as it immediately represents the indwelling divine power of Christ himself, which thrusts forward Christ's own word*" (CF §108.5). In this respect, "the basis of faith* must be for us the same as for the first Christians" (CF §128.2).

Individuals: See under Community*. In Schleiermacher's usage, the two terms are almost always mutually defining and interdependent, that is, dialectically related.

Infinite, the: Schleiermacher's famous, somewhat poetic definition of *religion* as "a sense and taste for the infinite in the finite" (in *OR* II) does not lead to "infinity" as an attribute of God in *Christian Faith*. The reason, as he says, is that the term is too negative and indefinite (*CF* §56.2; there he also rejects *unity* and *simplicity* for other reasons). *Infinity* refers to that which exists in contrast to whatever is finite, that is, "is co-determined by other things" (*CF* §56.2). As such, it rather serves as a feature of all the divine attributes, and it expresses the difference of divine causality* from all finite causality. In these two ways it nonetheless operates as a significant comparative term in Schleiermacher's talk about God.

Inner and outer: As a rule, organized phenomena, such as religion*, church*, and religious self-consciousness* possess dialectically* interrelated inner and outer (internal and external) features. *On Religion*, for example, is chiefly organized by this principle, which never translates into a distinction between what is essential and nonessential, though external aspects of the nature of an organized phenomenon do tend to be conceived as more changeable and transitory either in form or in specific content. The inner features of the Christian church, to give another example, tend to be relatively invariable, in this sense also "essential," whereas others are mutable (*CF* §§126-56).

Interconnectedness *(Zusammenhang)*: In ordinary German usage, this word often means "context" or "cohesiveness." For Schleiermacher, this key term almost always denotes "interconnectedness" (or, possibly "coinherence"). This is notably the case when he is referring to the natural order, where he conceives everything to be interconnected with everything else in theoretically ascertainable respects. It is not clear to what extent he finds room for pure chance within that order, though he does occasionally speak of "accidents" and "arbitrary" actions.

Questions for Reflection

The introduction of "chance," and sometimes of changing "process" into theism or into pantheism has led some scholars to affirm "panentheism," notably in process theology. In pantheism, of which Schleiermacher has been falsely accused, God's existing outside the natural order is taken to be inconceivable. Panentheism comes closer to his view that God reveals Godself only in and through the world God has created and preserves. However, in panentheism emphasis tends to be placed on God's being subject to change just as nature is. These are tough distinctions to work through. From what you've read thus far, how do you think he did this? Have you some sense of what questions about these positions might arise for you?

Jesus of Nazareth: This is Schleiermacher's way of identifying the historical Jesus. His lectures on the subject, *The Life of Jesus*, do not make the claim that an exact, integrated life story can be told by using the Gospel narratives, but they do establish the suitability of his life and work for his role of Redeemer*.

Joy *(Freude)*: One of the key ongoing affective states associated with the state of blessedness* is joy, especially evident in celebration of the birth and life of the Redeemer. See Prayer*.

Justification: Since the doctrine of justification was one of the most signal, complex, and contentious handed down by the Reformation, Schleiermacher was particularly keen on getting it right. Doing so was all the more challenging in that if the Lutheran and Reformed churches were to unite, as he devoutly hoped, they had to get clarity both on what united them in this respect and on where tolerable divergencies were still to be found. Structurally, his main strategy was to argue for the primacy of regeneration* and sanctification* and then use the doctrinal pair conversion* and justification to explain what regeneration consists of. "Being taken up into communion* with Christ in one's life, viewed as a human being's changed relationship to God, is that person's justification; viewed as a changed form of life, it is the person's conversion" (CF §107). Thus, "God's justifying the person who is converted includes God's forgiveness of the person's sins and recognizing the person as a child of God. However, this turning about in the person's relationship to God truly occurs only insofar as the person has genuine faith in the Redeemer*" (CF §109). For further explication see chapter 3 and Schleiermacher's 1830 sermon on "being made righteous" before God (Nicol 1997).

Knowing (Wissen): Dialectic* provides the basic principles for all inquiry in which the aim of thinking is knowing. This is a never-ending process but one in which it is possible to obtain well-grounded results. These results are usable, yet often they turn out to be temporary, subject to further investigation and testing (the pragmatic* aspect of Schleiermacher's critical realism). "Real knowing," as he calls it, is grounded in the real world. To obtain it requires an empirical* search for facts. Always and everywhere these so-called facts are to be sorted out, pulled together, and described or explained, and this aspect of the process of knowing requires a degree of speculation*, sometimes even before we can manage to get at the facts. The two aspects—empirical and speculative or rational—are mutually dependent. Finally, to be knowing is not invariably to have full and valid knowledge (*Erkenntnis*). Sometimes we simply have to live with that situation awhile, for we do not yet have everything we need at hand. Knowing is an uncertain but necessary adventure.

Leadership (Leitung): Leadership is a guiding, a leading forward and support, a moral responsibility on behalf of those who are led. Theology is done for the sake of those who lead in the church (*Kirchenleitung*), and the crown of all such leading and allied cooperative effort in the church, whether by clergy or laity, is care* of souls (*Seelenleitung*), the basic subject matter of practical* theology.

Love: See God* in chapter 3. As in popular usage then and now, Schleiermacher employs several meanings of *love*, hence attention to context is of critical importance.

Magical thinking: This extreme way of thinking views the divine activity in Christ or the church as like a "magic spell." That is, an instance of this activity is attributed to the person yet is "not mediated by anything natural"; thus, it appears to be "purely accidental," not part of a larger reality. The consequence of such thinking is a tendency "to destroy all naturalness in the continuing activity of Christ" (CF §§101.3-4). In Christology this tendency is associated with docetic heresy and with what has been called a "pipeline" view of grace*.

Metaphysics: Although Schleiermacher thrived in the era of German idealism, he refused to be strictly an idealist, adopting pragmatic, critical realist theories of meaning and truth* instead. In his day, as chiefly since the very beginnings of philosophy, metaphysics was mainly ontology, the theory and investigation into being (*ontos*) in general. His dialectic includes some of this interest, but he was chary of making truth claims about transcendent reality. This is why he sought to extirpate "metaphysics" from the domain of theology and to eradicate any effort to identify religion itself as a worldview in this sense, focusing instead on feeling*. He was also canny enough to realize that no one is likely totally to succeed in these tasks. Metaphysics conceived as a discipline of philosophy also has other functions, in which elements of his thinking can still be contributive, namely an examination, critique, and clarification (1) of presuppositions* that in practice underlie concepts, judgments, and ways of defining reality, (2) of principles that do or can provide the grounding for fields of study, (3) of bridges between philosophical concerns and the sciences, and (4) of how interdisciplinary study is to be constituted (the latter a set of functions scarcely underway even now).

Ministry (*Dienst*, service): Equally of clergy and laity (see ch. 3). In the fullest sense, worship is *Gottesdienst* (being in the service of God).

Miracle (*Wunder*): If miracles (and supposed fulfillment of prophecies) were ever important for demonstrating that Jesus was and is the Redeemer, which Schleiermacher holds to be quite dubious, the continuation of his work by the Holy Spirit brought that expectation to an end. In his view, when conceived as discrete invasions of the natural order by some superior or transcendent power, miracles play no significant role in Christianity. On the one hand, given a Christian view of the divine creation-preservation and government* of the world, every natural event is a miracle. On the other hand, the only true miracle in the first sense is Jesus' becoming the Redeemer and inaugurator of the reign of God via his complete God-consciousness* and sinless perfection*. These views may be traced especially in *Christian Faith* §§14.3, 47.1, 76.2, 93.3, 99.2, 103.1 and 4, 108.5, 117.2, 123.2, 124.3, and 130.4.

Moral: See Community* and Ethics*. Morals (*Sitte*) provide the subject matter for this reflective discipline (*Ethik, Sittenlehre*). An action may be called "moral" either by custom or by individual judgment or by ethics.

Mystery and mysticism: Schleiermacher prefers not to use these words to discuss theological matters, regarding them to be chiefly outsiders' lingo for authentic Christian experience that they have not had and cannot grasp. However, in rare instances they do appear in *Christian Faith* as indicators of such experience, in order roughly to distinguish it from two extreme, inappropriate ways of thinking about Christian experience that he terms magical* and empirical*. They refer to a "middle way," which involves having "a real experience of living community* with Christ" (CF §101.4) and which leads to an acknowledgment that the supernatural is always becoming natural in such experience. That is, the divine really does work redemptively in and through natural conditions and not otherwise. The Word becomes flesh. *On Religion* presents a different picture, for there Schleiermacher is addressing mostly outsiders. In all five discourses we find highly important indicators of the authentic "middle way" of Christian experience. In *On Religion* I, he holds up a "higher priesthood" that "loves the highest and eternal in the very midst of earthly life" and "proclaims the inner meaning of all spiritual mysteries" (46). At the opening of *On Religion* II, he asks his readers to prepare themselves in solemn stillness to be "initiated" into "mysteries" (67), later speaking of presentiments* of mystery in nature (117), and he says that "tirelessly eternal humanity is bringing light out of its mysterious inner being and presenting itself within the ever changing process of finite life in a multitude of different forms" (123). In *On Religion* III, he rails against the stifling of children's sense for mystery (185) and against denigration of "the innermost heart of human being." In contrast, "the heroes of religion" are those who have not succumbed to these pressures, "who have experienced its innermost mysteries" (194). In *On Religion* IV, he continues: in the religious association between leader and congregation "holy mysteries are then bound to be discovered and celebrated—mysteries, if rightly conceived, that are not merely significant emblems but natural indications of a distinctly formed consciousness and of quite definite perceptions" (212). Finally, in *On Religion* V, as in *Christian Faith*, he avers that "every beginning in religion, as elsewhere, is full of mystery" (315) and that "the mysterious reality of religion" can be addressed in every conceivable mode (322). Admittedly, this is rhapsodic discourse, in which much leeway can be permitted, but it intends to go deep.

Questions for Reflection

In *Die Mystk und das Wort* (1924) and other places the noted Swiss Reformed theologian Emil Brunner (1889–1966) falsely excoriated Schleiermacher for taking a heretically "mystical" approach to Christian doctrine. That year Brunner's countryman Karl Barth (1886–1968) responded: "No, that's going way too far!" In the early 1960s Barth told me that Schleiermacher had been his "first love" and that in his own rather trenchant criticisms of Schleiermacher's theology he had rather been bent on opposing the great churchman's camp followers. In 1968 he produced a list of possible changes of mind. (See my account in Duke and Streetman 1988). Today some leading Barthians are finding the two greats to be much closer than had been thought. In my view, such intense miscues and changes of interpretation are due as much to inadequate reading habits as to biases, mimicking of trends, or rhetorical combat. What possibilities of this sort do you see in yourself? For help, I recommend Mortimer Adler's much noted *How to Read a Book*.[6]

Nature (Natur): The entire natural world is an interconnected whole*, including human nature, even though it is not static but changing.

Nature (Wesen): In ordinary German usage sometimes this term means "essence" but very rarely in Schleiermacher's discourse except for the adjectival *wesentlich* ("essential"). With reference to God, *höchste Wesen* means "Supreme Being." With reference to virtually everything else—for example, *Wesen der Religion* (OR II)—it means "nature," which implies its overall defining characteristics, not some primary set of them in comparison with which the others are deemed incidental. Accordingly, the entirety of the five discourses *On Religion*, not the second discourse exclusively, outline the nature of religion. All five sets of characteristics set forth there are "essential."

Organic, organization: The perceptible* world* presents itself organically, as complex sets of interconnected* parts, for which the term *organization* is used. Everything in this organic world is subject to contrast* in the judgments we form of it (all judgments of discrimination, not simply evaluative judgments). A view formed contrary to this understanding of the world* is termed *mechanistic*.

Original (*urbildlich*): This term stands for what is originative ideally or on a sustained basis, not simply what started something off temporally. Not seeing this can mislead one in reading, for example, of Christ's "original" nature or of "the original perfection of the world" (*CF* §59) or that of "humanity" (*CF* §§60-61) or of "original sin" (*CF* §§70-72).

Orthodox and **Heterodox:** Both terms should be honorific, given the limited historical sense in which doctrines of the church tend to transmogrify from each side to the other and may gain currency* somewhere in that process (*BO* §§203-11; *CF* §25 P.S. and §131.2).

Perception: For the several levels of usage for *Anschauung* see chapter 2. The orientation of *Wahrnehmung*, by contrast, is always focused on the senses, hence is rendered "sense perception."

Perfection, completeness, consummation (*Vollendung*): In Schleiermacher's discourse this term tends to denote not so much finality as a model or ideal state to reach for.

Personal existence (*Persönlichkeit*): Although, in later German usage especially, this word can mean "personality," it never means this in Schleiermacher's discourse. It should be rendered "personal existence" instead. Usually *-keit* holds a range of meanings associated with "-ness," as in *Heiligkeit* ("holiness," having a holy quality or a holy existence). Thus, *Persönlichkeit* refers to one's existing as a person, bearing the distinctive quality of personhood, not specifically having a particular type of "personality," as we would say. Schleiermacher thus attributes "personal existence" to Christ based on the "person-forming" activity of God in his life.

Philosophical theology: See Apologetics* and chapter 2. This one of theology's three parts is geared internally to the church, not externally. Its aim is to bring philosophical mindedness (Tice 2003) and general scholarly perspectives to bear on strictly theological concerns. Schleiermacher strenuously resists importation of philosophical content into theological views (*BO* §§32-68 and so on).

Philosophy (*Philosophie, Weltweisheit*): See Dialectic*.

Piety (*Frömmigkeit*):[7] *Piety*, which from a Christian point of view is conceived as "the basis of all religious communities" and, "regarded purely in and of itself," is "a distinct formation of feeling*, or of immediate self-consciousness" (*CF* §3; see ch. 2). As such, piety is "the highest stage of human self-consciousness" and is "distinguished from all other feelings," though "in its actual occurrence" it is never disconnected from the immediately "lower stage" of sensory consciousness, that is, is never wholly inorganic (*CF* §5). Now, the distinct formation of feeling in piety is this: "That we are conscious of ourselves as absolutely dependent*, or, which intends the same meaning, as being in relation with God." All these elements and qualifications that belong to piety are "essential" to human nature. Moreover, "in its development*" this set of characteristics "necessarily becomes community* as well," community that is both uneven and fluid and "distinctly circumscribed—that is, church." This concise restatement of Schleiermacher's view is wholly represented in propositions 3-6 of *Christian Faith*, as indicated, and is further explicated in the sections beneath them. When added to in §§7-14, they reflect the same unfolding of definition as that already presented in the five discourses *On Religion*. In effect, *piety*, thus defined, is a synonym for "faith*," and it is treated in the same way. Schleiermacher's exposition of each, moreover, can be subject to similar misunderstandings. Notably, although in *Christian Faith* §3 he clearly indicates that *piety* is not to be made identical with "a knowledge or a doing," it is also true that in the necessary context of communal involvement the distinct feeling of piety must find expression in both knowing and doing, though always to some extent in an embodied, sensory manner. Second, although he highlights the feeling of absolute dependence* here and throughout *Christian Faith* as the way we register being in a living relationship with God, we must always be on the lookout for damaging tendencies to reduce piety to a kind of knowing or doing, so that "piety" would be denoted by correct belief ("the letter") or a prescribed behavior (the law). It cannot be repeated too often that in themselves these things do not yield to us a living faith, true piety, or, as Christians, the genuine feeling of being in a redemptive* relationship with God. Third, not all other stages of piety within non-Christian or even Christian communities of faith contain the feeling* of being *absolutely* dependent. Finally, *dependent* does not mean "dependency," which would imply an unfree, slavish relationship, not the "liberty of the children of God" (one of his favorite uses of a biblical phrase[8]). As Christians we are absolutely dependent, but this feature of the relationship also enlivens us to be responsive, self-active, and free.

Positive: Distinctively "located" (placed, posited) in social practice or in the subject matter of the positive sciences (law, theology, medicine).

Practical theology: See Leadership*. All Evangelical Christian theology is supposed to be done for the sake of leadership in the church. Practical theology focuses on the carrying out of such leadership, or its *praxis* within the community of faith, whereas Christian ethics* surveys principles for the entire Christian life. Roles and relations in regard to society and the state are considered in both of these overlapping domains. The closest Schleiermacher himself comes to a separate critical examination of societal relations is in church statistics*. Only in philosophy does he fully treat of the state, though related material is to be found in his courses on all these other subjects, as in *On Religion*.

Pragmatic: See under Currency* and Knowing*. In detail, Schleiermacher's views on knowing, history, meaning, and truth and those among twentieth-century pragmatists, especially John Dewey, are very much alike. All four interests, for him, are to be understood developmentally and contextually, but this does not entail that carrying on the search toward an ultimate goal (reason in its final, consensual attainment) is meaningless.

Prayer (Gebet): In the Christian context, all prayer boils down to a will for, or devotion (*Ergebung*) to, the reign of God, that is, to fulfillment of the promise inherent in Christ's mission and to an expression of grateful acknowledgment of God's sovereignty, grace, and glory (cf. CF §47.1), that is, to giving thanks for all that God has done and continues to do. Consistent with this attitude, there is room for yearning and hope as well, though these cannot be expressions of Christian* immediate self-consciousness, for they pertain to the future. Petitions may be well-meaning, but they often tend wrongly to be mere wishes or to contain faulty, even magical*, expectations from our relationship with God. Moreover, it would be improper to expect to influence God to change whatever order has already been established by God or to expect any strictly reciprocal response from God (see Questions* under Interconnectedness*). Prayer is proper only when we are fulfilling our Christian calling*. It may not be a substitute for work. Prayer is most in tune when it bears the calling and welfare of the entire church in mind. Accordingly, it is expressed not out of mere piousness (*pietas* vs. piety* or faith*) or selfish interest. In fine, through "joy* in God," authentic Christian prayer ultimately yields an unalloyed "rest" (*Ruhe*), or being at peace (*Friede*), in God. See especially *Christian Faith* §§146-47.

Preparatory grace: See God-consciousness* and Grace*. This traditional term includes, but is not restricted to, periods before Jesus enters history or individual lives.

Presentation (*Darstellung*): Literally, "putting it out there," a style of discourse chosen for reports, sermons, and accounts of faith-doctrine, among other things. In Schleiermacher's usage this word is not appropriately rendered "re-presentation" (*Vorstellung*, a word he also regularly uses for "notions" in contrast to more solid "ideas" or "principles"). It is a function especially of honest, well-grounded, well-ordered, carefully thought out communication*.

Presentiment (*Ahnung*): This is a preliminary, partially formed sense or hint of something that is to come or already exists in fuller form but is only vaguely apprehended. One may hold a presentiment of faith*.

Presupposition (*Voraussetzung*): Typically, as part of his historical-critical approach to inquiry, Schleiermacher is very attentive to these preformed, sometimes unconsciously held suppositions that are posited in, and thus underlie, experiences, claims, arguments, and choices of terms. Generally, presuppositions are, therefore, to be differentiated from assumptions (*Annehmen*) contained in an argument or postulates in a mathematical presentation. In its entirety, part 1 of *Christian Faith* comprises "explication of religious self-consciousness as it is constantly presupposed by, but also constantly contained in, every Christian religious affective state" (heading before §32). Thus, what is explicated there is held to be posited in, and thus to underlie, authentically Christian faith experiences, though this material is not directly expressed in it because it is simply preposited in the formation of the affective states that refer to "the redemption accomplished through Jesus of Nazareth" (CF §11). This material is also "contained in" those affective states, however; hence, part 1 is also comprised of genuine propositions regarding Christian faith.

Proclamation (*Verkündigung*): Sometimes Schleiermacher uses this key term as a synonym for *preaching (Predigten)*, but it generally has a much broader meaning. Jesus' "self-proclamation," which set off the entire Christian story, occurred in both word and deed, in the influence of both his "person" and his "work." The same is true in the passing down of what he started within the Christian community and its "common spirit*" from generation to generation. Thus, as in the Hebrew *dabar* (word), the Word* and the "ministry of the Word of God" (CF §§133-35) are active; they are not restricted even in sermons to explication of scripture, though—as in Schleiermacher's sermons— that is a basic ingredient. Proclamation is active testimony, engaging witness.

Proof: Proofs occur in demonstrative arguments. In that sense, Schleiermacher consistently holds to the position that such proofs do not prove anything of import for Christian doctrine. They do not prove the existence of God. They do not suffice to lead anyone to faith in Christ. Accordingly, he eschews use of so-called proof-texts lifted from scripture. In the numerous instances when he cites biblical passages, this practice is meant to indicate what he is talking about. Sometimes it also displays a significant rootage in the biblical witness. It is never intended to serve as an authority standing by itself to provide proof. Accordingly, Schleiermacher does not regard deductive systems of theology to be very authentic or compelling.

Prophetic doctrine: Such doctrine (CF §§157-63) refers to future possibilities, not to immediate religious self-consciousness (ch. 2). Thus, it bears no status as regular doctrine regarding faith. Talk about "last things," for example, can be nothing more than an expression of yearning or hope. Christian faith and life are not, and cannot be, grounded in any of it, whether scripture contains references to it or not. Strictly speaking, such explicit references to the future "consummation of the church" do not belong to the canon* of scripture, though they are interestingly embedded in it. As in most matters, however, Schleiermacher is tolerant of the presence of such notions in church life, despite their relative inappropriateness from a dogmatic* standpoint.

Questions for Reflection

Some critics would claim that Schleiermacher's overall approach to theology not only depends overmuch on irrational, "subjective," and "practical" components of faith (feeling, self-consciousness) but also relies too little on "rational" grounds, proofs, and theoretical perspectives. Others argue that he is not "practical" enough, that is, does not provide direct rules for moral life. Based on what you have read here thus far, where might you stand in relation to these criticisms? If theology has to do with "faith seeking understanding" (Anselm), how do you think you are to gain the understanding you need and for what purpose?

Providence (Vorsehung): In a broad sense, Schleiermacher has a doctrine of providence, which would hold up the promise and tell the story of God's creative guiding and protective presence in human history. However, he prefers not to use the word, in part because it suggests particular events of God's activity existing independently of the divine government* of the world as a whole* (CF §164.3). The ideas of a single eternal divine decree* and of two periods (of a sort) within the course of human history—one period of "preparatory and introductory" activity, on the one hand, and the other period of "development and fulfillment," on the other hand—suffice (§164.2).

Psychology: As we have seen, psychological concepts are a major supportive ingredient in Schleiermacher's theological projects. Expectably, these concepts were generated on a strong empirical* basis but are also structured by impressively innovative speculative* elements. While his lectures on psychology (trans. Lawler, in preparation) largely bear the characteristics familiar in philosophy of mind today, the rest of what he borrows for use in theology appears in ethics*, philosophy of education* (*Pädagogik*) and other places, including theology itself. All this is yet to be pieced together, though it is already clear that his work brings important contributions, even correctives, to present-day inquiry and practice (see Tice, "Schleiermacher's Psychology," 1991). Moreover, in a second essay (not yet published), I attempt to show that his psychology, alongside his dialectic* (which includes logic), provides a ground for a complex organization of philosophy and of its bridge functions in relation to all the scientific disciplines. Rarely has the unfinished work of a thinker borne such power for future studies beyond his or her own thought.

Receptivity and **self-initiated activity** *(Selbsttätigkeit, Spontaneität)*: The concept of self-initiated activity, frequently met in Schleiermacher's discourse, is dialectically* paired with *receptivity (Empfänglichkeit, Receptivität)*. Since they constitute reciprocal elements in human experience, it is important to analyze what they consist of in any given experience. In general, one would not expect to meet one aspect without the other. See chapter 2.

Redemption, Redeemer *(Erlösung, Erlöser)*: Literally, this figurative word means "being released" or "set free." So, Christ* the *Erlöser* is the one through whom God liberates those who have been in bondage to "the collective life of sin*," and he releases them into the "collective life of grace*." This is Schleiermacher's sense of the matter. However, in both languages the word also suggests a cross-centered view of that process, one that draws upon the multiple images of atonement* on the cross to be found in the Scriptures, and this procedure he does not accept. Rather, he critiques these views, finds them to be misleading and inadequate, and retains the broader meanings of being set free and released. Now, since the help given cannot consist of restoring one to a previously better condition, the release is from a condition in which the higher self-consciousness is obstructed but the possibility of God-consciousness* being introduced into one's life exists nonetheless. Once this process has begun to happen, for a time, a resultant state that can arise is one Schleiermacher calls "God-forgetfulness" (CF §11.2). In contrast to the other monotheisms (CF §10), only in Christianity is redemption its "main business," the "focal point" of piety*. Only there is the original and continuing activity of Christ "the primary element" (CF §11.4). See Christ* and Decree*.

Reflection *(Reflection)*: This is a chiefly cognitive act of looking closely at and thinking in an orderly way about a subject; sometimes it is a synonym for *Betrachtung**.

Regeneration: See Blessedness*, Conversion*, Justification*, Sin*. The term means, literally, "rebirth" or "new life."

Reign of God *(Reich Gottes)*: God's sovereign government* of the world in Christ is highlighted in this concept, which Schleiermacher frequently uses. For him, it never had to be rendered in the long familiar phrase "kingdom of God," which smacks of undue anthropomorphizing, unnecessarily narrow political imagery, and an exclusively male gender identity for God. Since the church* represents the communal form of the advancing reign of God, in its ideal conception the church is often simply identified by him as the reign of God, which God not only inaugurated but also brings to fruition and sustains in its coexistence with the rest of the human world*.

Religion *(Religion)*: Piety* is the innermost core of *religion*, a term that captures all the internal and external features of the phenomenon (see *Inner* and *outer*). Accordingly, Schleiermacher reserves *religion* to indicate that fully orbed phenomenon. *On Religion* is the place where he works out all of its principle features. The idea of Christianity* presents the most completely developed* form of religion thus far. In its many and varied permutations it is to be viewed as "a religion."

Religious *(fromm, religiöse)*: See Piety*.

Revealed: See Revelation in chapter 2. Schleiermacher's theology centers on divine revelation but it neither narrowly restricts nor leaves entirely open how that revealing activity of God is registered and received and taken up by persons.

Sacrament: For the sake of convenience only, Schleiermacher tentatively adopts the word *sacrament* for the two rites of baptism and the Lord's Supper, finding no historical significance of the word outside the Roman Catholic Church and viewing these two rites simply as continuations of Christ's priestly activity in the church. In this sense, they play important roles as essential elements of the church's ongoing life. See *Christian Faith* §§136-42 and especially the appendix to them (§143).

Sanctification: See Blessedness*, Justification*, Sin*. This term refers to the process of being made holy and living a holy life in relationship to God.

Science (Wissenschaft): In Schleiermacher's discourse *science* is a supremely honorific term, not to be confused with *scholarship*, though he would have liked all scholarly effort to bear the marks of the highly organized, sophisticated activity he calls "science." He does not privilege natural science in his accounts of what science should be. Nor are the main ingredients of the natural and the human sciences greatly different, in his view. In an essay based on extensive investigations I had made into the history of science (Richardson 1991), I have suggested that in general terms and apart from the special investment people might have in particular sciences outside theology, Schleiermacher had a more adequate, systematic, and thoroughgoing conception of science than perhaps any other scholar in his century. There is not space to outline the reasons here. Some of the reasons relate to his grasp of what it takes to think about various aspects of what is (being) with an aim of knowing* (dialectic*). Some have to do with his profound, pragmatic, and practical sense for the interconnectedness* of nature and others with his occupation with well-formed methods of inquiry and associated rules of procedure, not all of them purely "empirical*." Still others focus on his keen awareness of ethical* and values* issues that arise at all levels and in all areas of scientific work. Some derive from his prescient vision of interdisciplinary inquiry in universities and refer to the essential roles philosophy* can play in the constitution of scientific disciplines and in their interaction. Finally, important ingredients that I did not treat at that time reflect his highly innovative grasp of hermeneutics* and the arts of criticism*, both of which bear potential impacts on the conduct of all science. Theology* promises to be a field of study unusually blessed with Schleiermacher's occupations regarding science, notably through his *Brief Outline of Theology as a Field of Study* and his pursuit of most major areas in this field. Above all, he was a pioneer in the studied awareness that science is an extremely refined and complex matter, the components of which are subject to rapid change, therefore that science cannot be simply defined. This awareness still flies in the face of summary efforts to define science in science textbooks today.

Questions for Reflection

From where have you gotten the view of science you carry? In what way does that view serve your need to understand faith, and where do you find it to be inadequate for helping to answer to that need? Does science include psychology for you?

Self-consciousness (Selbstbewusstsein): See *Christian* religious immediate self-consciousness.

Separation, sectarianism, schism, heresy: Schleiermacher was an ecumenical theologian. He tried to issue and answer the call to cooperation and unity particularly among churches born of the Reformation. He directed his theological work and allied activity as a church leader* especially to effecting union between the Lutheran and Reformed churches in Germany. Among other things, this effort required combating the contrary activities listed here: separatism, sectarianism, schism, and heresy. See *Brief Outline* and Nicol 1997 and 2004.

Sin: Sin is composed of being out of a salutary relationship with God and therefore being in need of redemption*. In dogmatics* Schleiermacher rarely speaks of particular sins because he does not view them as transgression of any law or as want of conformity to any law. What is critical is one's overall status in relation to God. Moreover, until one is reborn, or regenerated*, to the new life in Christ one belongs to "the collective life of sin*," which has two aspects to it, both insofar as one is engaged in relation to other human beings or oneself and interacts with the world that God has created and preserved. The first aspect is original sin, which is passed down through these relations, not by procreation. Socially speaking, we inherit this aspect. The second aspect is actual sin, which is one's own self-active contribution (see Receptivity*) to the collective life of sin. In every instance, our sin is an admixture of the two aspects. In redemption, summarized in the processes of regeneration* and sanctification*, God forgives our sin and restores us to a right relationship, that is, justifies* us, or makes us righteous in God's sight. This happens by our being ushered into the collective life of grace*, by the power of the Holy Spirit* in the church. Grace* makes us conscious of our sin; thus, that consciousness is not a first step to our being conscious of redemption in Christ. Nor is nonmoral evil in the world a punishment for the sin of human beings (see Evil*). However, we are thereby made conscious of God as holy and just. In the sense that God creates human beings with free will, and has ordained sin as a prior condition for redemption, God is the author of sin. See *Christian Faith* §§65-85 and chapter 3 here.

Species-consciousness (*Gattungsbewusstsein*): In the development of human nature it is essential that one form a consciousness that we are all members of the human race, part of the larger humanity, each in one's own way (see ch. 1). This consciousness becomes a building block for a fully constructed awareness that we participate in the collective life of sin* and of grace*, also that each person bears responsibility for the well-being of all nature and humanity.

Speculative and empirical: See Empirical* thinking, Psychology*. Although empirical and speculative elements of inquiry are distinctly different by definition, they are to some degree inseparable both ideally and in practice. Often, however, speculation tends inappropriately to fly away from organic reality into some far-fetched theoretical ideal, whereas empirical investigation may easily lose the quality of interconnectedness that speculative effort might help supply.

Spirit (*Geist*): As in Christian tradition generally, Schleiermacher conceives of God and human beings as capable of mutual communication because both are spirit. However, in his psychology* he does not view the human body and spirit as separable. The two together he calls "psyche."

Statistics, church: Schleiermacher contrived this major discipline of theology, on which he lectured, to be the historical study of the contemporary church in its internal constitution and external relations (BO §§232-50). Despite the name Schleiermacher assigned to it, this discipline, like all others in theology, is at its best when it combines religious interest with a scientific* spirit and intends to serve leadership* of the church. For other ages "symbolics" and "biblical dogmatics" are closer to church statistics, as directed to a specific period and locale, than to dogmatics*, and thus far they tend to be more chronological than properly historical. Today a great deal that goes by the name of "theology" is actually what Schleiermacher called church statistics.

Subjectivity and objectivity: By virtue of the way human beings are constituted, these two features of mental functioning are dialectically* related, two aspects of the same activity though in comparatively varying degrees. Instead of calling a view or phenomenon purely objective or subjective, it is more accurate and fruitful to inquire about the degree to which it emphasizes the one or the other.

Supernatural: God's coming into nature occurs from a supernatural position, that is, from beyond nature, as in Christ* (see miracle*) and redemption* by grace*. However, God manifests Godself only in and through the world*, so that God's supernatural being can be experienced and known only in this manner (economically) not in itself (immanently, *in se*).

Supreme Being *(höchstes Wesen)*: This is a designation for God, reflecting the biblical name "Highest."

System(atic): This concept reflects the interconnectedness* of a subject area in at once a corresponding and cohesive fashion, constructing it in such a way that each distinguishable part is made conceptually transparent to every other part. In general, the urge to systematize, or to synthesize what is analyzed, is a feature of every genuinely scientific* endeavor, in contrast to forming mere aggregates. Systems should be open-ended, to allow for alteration in the light of new knowledge or information. In theological science, it is inappropriate to try to provide a system deductively (see Proof*) because of the complex and changing historical nature of the subject matter. This danger of underestimating the historical character of dogmatics*, plus the danger of overlooking its aim to serve church leadership*, led Schleiermacher to avoid using *systematic theology* as the name for that discipline as a whole (BO §97).

Teleological: *Telos* means end, purpose, or goal. Teleological ethics is that which considers morals preeminently in the light of such characteristics. Teleological religion does the same with religion, in the case of Christianity focusing on the divine purpose of redemption* through Christ and the resultant reign* of God* in and through the church*. The development* of humanity toward these ideal states is a key feature of Schleiermacher's understanding of Christianity. In *Christian Faith* §§9-11 Schleiermacher introduces a very elaborate inquiry into the marks that could distinguish one religion from another, an inquiry more formal than that found in *On Religion* V. At the level of monotheism, he depicts the pervasive influence upon affective states in Islam to lie in its subordination of active, moral capacities to passive, natural ones, the result of which he terms *aesthetic religion*. There piety comes to rest in a set of "immutable divine appointments." In this respect, he holds, Islam is closer to polytheism than to the other two major monotheistic religions. Of these two, Judaism is teleological in that passive, natural ends are subordinated to active, moral ends. This characteristic he sums up in the notion of a "commanding divine will contained in the law, to which the affective states of piety are subjected." In a more complete sense

Christianity is also teleological, but the affective states of piety are entirely focused on "activity in the reign of God" and more passive states all denote a "transition" to that activity.

Questions for Reflection

Does this analysis mean that Schleiermacher has broken his own rule and simply identified the Judaic and Christian religions with morality? This was certainly not his intent, as his references to "affective states" shows; also, he assigns versions of the basic feeling of absolute dependence to all three monotheistic religions. In any case, the pertinent "ends" are not all moral. Moreover, it is entirely consistent with his other accounts of religion, regarded as feeling, to notice that certain moral ends that suffuse the entire expression of Judaic and Christian religions actually issue forth from their affective components. Yet, it is not yet made clear among the definitions presented thus far how his accounts of Christian faith and of the Christian life are to relate to each other. How do you think they might relate? How do they relate in your own thinking and on what grounds? See "Christian Ethics" in chapter 3.

Theology: Evangelical theology, as Schleiermacher conceived of it in his epoch-making work *Brief Outline of Theology as a Field of Study* (1811, 1830), is composed of three wholly interdependent parts: philosophical, historical, and practical theology. All three parts are pursued for the purpose of leadership* in the church. All other disciplines associated with theological work, that is, linguistic and strictly chronological studies, are simply auxiliary to theology itself. None of the three parts is quite what their titles might indicate, for Schleiermacher has reinterpreted each one. Moreover, the interrelationships among them are very complex and are often sadly left unexamined by interpreters. For brief initial explanations see chapter 1, also Philosophical*, Historical*, and Practical*, also Apologetics*, Dogmatics*, Ethics*, Exegetical*, and Statistics*. Among the three parts, philosophical theology is largely analytical and preliminary but not foundational; historical theology comprises the main body and includes disciplines such as dogmatics normally not thought of as strictly historical heretofore; practical theology is the "crown" of the entire enterprise.

Trinity (*Dreiheit, Dreifaltigkeit*): Both German terms are set in contrast to *Einheit* (oneness). The second term means "threefoldness," which could be interpreted to refer simply to a "threeness" of *hypostases* or *personae* in God or to God's being active in a threefold mode or manner, which latter conception could likewise mean that in God's oneness God acts all at once, as it were, but always in a threefold way. Alternatively, if God is seen to act in a threefold mode or manner, this could mean that God always acts in accordance with "the one eternal divine decree" of creation, preservation, and redemption but in an unfolding development to be viewed for theological purposes in historical perspective. The latter alternative position is as close to a fully warranted, reasonable position as Schleiermacher could get, given all the limits that the theological method to which he subscribed required. Accordingly, *Christian Faith* is organized in the following "triune" way. Part 1 represents what is "presupposed" in Christian consciousness of divine redemption through Jesus concerning the one God's relationship with human beings in and through the world. Therein this world is taken as a whole and is viewed as created and preserved by God. Part 2 then presents that very same

God pointedly with respect to divine grace (versus sin) viewed as it has appeared in the Redeemer and still does appear by the Holy Spirit in the church (as its "common spirit," i.e., "Christ in us") and through the church into the rest of the world. All of this doctrine, when taken to be about God's relationship to human beings—collectively, singly, and in our participation in the world as a whole—is summed up in the conclusion "Regarding the Divine Trinity (*Dreiheit*)." He calls this section the "capstone" of the roofline over the entire doctrinal edifice, however problematic formulations concerning the triune God might be. See also "The Triune God" in chapter 3.

Truth and error: Truth, according to Schleiermacher's critically realist and pragmatic view, is never absolute or certain. Outside mathematical systems he expected to find some error in every truth and some truth in every error. Nevertheless, he held that there is sufficient evidence to suggest an ideal situation in which the joint agreement of rational minds would achieve a maximum of truth, which is a way of affirming that progress in what is discovered by reason can be achieved. One underlying presupposition* of these claims is the belief that God's world is open to scrutiny by human beings as one interconnected* whole*. A task of the sciences is to work toward an apprehension of that whole through a gradually more complete mastery of lesser wholes. He does not presuppose that wholes are unchanging in their composition or content.

Universe (*Universum*): In *On Religion* and some other places, he uses this term (which has also passed into English from Latin) to stand for the whole interconnectedness of nature. It is possible to have an *Anschauung** of this *Universum*, if only incompletely. This perception is closely associated with the feeling* of absolute dependence on God but must not be mistaken for it.

Validity (*Geltung*): See Currency*.

Value (*Wert*): At age twenty-four Schleiermacher produced a sizeable essay presenting a general theory of value, not published in full until 1984 (Lawler and Tice 1995). Wilhelm Dilthey had issued a scattered fourth of it in 1870. This subject area was not a noticeable discipline of philosophy until late in the century, and he never took it up again in systematic fashion except indirectly in his ethical* writings. Among its still remarkable features is its overcoming the strict bifurcation between fact and value regnant since the seventeenth century and obdurately retained even today. Facts and values he took to be mutually dependent modes of discernment, present in all of observed life. The theory also offers a well-argued alternative to happiness, economic goods, and utilitarian gains as broadly popular but faulty measures of value in human life. It does so, moreover, in a way that does not center on what is quantified. This richly endowed, clever piece carries much merit for enhancing current inquiry into values. As a "New Year's gift," it is the closest predecessor to his 1800 *Soliloquies* (Tice, forthcoming), which was also a gift for the turn of the year. Lawler has also edited a fine collection of *Fifteen Sermons* by Schleiermacher delivered at the New Year (2004), a moment of importance for self-evaluation.

Wehmut: This term means melancholy or "tugging sadness and longing." For Schleiermacher it is always admixed with joy* among the regenerate and is a "keynote" of Christian sensibility. See Blessedness*.

Whole (*Ganze*): In thinking about both physical and historical reality, Schleiermacher displays a tendency to consider relations between parts and wholes. These relations are significant aspects of what now exists, but their configurations can change, and they are almost bound to do so. Thus, he speaks of the world* as a whole that can be broken down into discernable parts, and he seeks to grasp what kinds of relations are in play between these parts and the universal whole. The Christian church is a whole, unfortunately separated into parts, and the corresponding question is, *how can we learn both to live with these differences and to seek desirable change?* All of human history and society is composed of such inherently flexible configurations between parts and whole. So are fields of study, and so forth. See *Brief Outline of Theology as a Field of Study* for examples of these configurations.

Word: The word is whatever God proclaims in Christ. Schleiermacher uses this term of scripture only insofar as it represents and serves this purpose. "Ministry of the Word" refers precisely to this word. The word become flesh is God's word spoken and enacted in Christ, not a preexistent part of the Godhead become incarnate*. "The word became flesh" is God's word proclaimed by word and deed by and through the Redeemer*.

World: For the most part, *world* means that human world to which religious self-consciousness can refer on planet Earth. Since human beings are part of the interconnectedness* of both physical and human nature, the physical world is included by implication. However, Schleiermacher does not speak of the redemption of physical nature as such, nor does he speak of a cosmic Christ. The church coexists alongside the rest of this human world and for the sake of this world. Environmental consciousness of the kind with which we are familiar today was not his strong suit. He was not totally oblivious of environmental responsibility either, but his approach was grounded on the view that we are stewards of the earth.

Questions for Reflection

These final items especially demonstrate how vast, intricately complex, and all-encompassing Schleiermacher's open but systematic discourse was, both inside and outside theology. Yet, he always sought to protect theology's distinctiveness from philosophy and from speculation that is divorced from empirical/historical investigation or divorced from the other sciences. He does selectively "borrow" from the other sciences to serve mostly introductory aims. How do you think one might undertake to pursue such activities in relation to theology today? What would enter into configurations of knowledge or insight that Schleiermacher could not have formed, given the limited knowledge or sociopolitical circumstances of his day? In turn, how nearly consistent might these be—for example, those that could be borrowed from physical science or psychoanalytic/developmental psychology or political philosophy—with Schleiermacher's main perspectives and insights? Finally, do you see ways in which such considerations could affect your forming theology for yourself? Would you do this without making the product into a strictly individual theology, which Schleiermacher himself abjured? Why would you want to heed his warning that a theologian must seek to understand and purvey only what the "common spirit" of the church viewed as a community of faith conveys, not simply proclaim one's own constructions? Or, why would you set this warning aside?

NOTES

1. Schleiermacher's Life and Context

1. See my accounts on this founding in Herbert Richardson, ed., *Friedrich Schleiermacher and the Founding of the University of Berlin: The Study of Religion as a Scientific Discipline* (Lewiston, N.Y.: Edwin Mellen, 1991), in my English translation of his *Occasional Thoughts on Universities in the German Sense* (San Francisco: Edwin Mellen, 1991, 2005), and in my forthcoming volume with Edwina Lawler, containing his *Writings on Academia*.

2. *Br.* I, 294.

3. *Br.* IV (Dec. 17, 1809), 173; cf. also *Br.* IV, 87.

4. E.g. cf. *Br.* IV, 610-11 (1827).

5. *Br.* IV, 87; cf. also *Br.* I, 14.

6. *On the Glaubenslehre*, p. 66 (my trans.).

7. See *Soliloquies*, 85.

8. *Br.* I, 10.

9. *Soliloquies*, 74; cf. *Br.* I, 11 (here "spirit" refers to an act both spiritual and intellectual).

10. *Soliloquies*, 40.

11. *Br.* I, 53.

12. *Br.* I, 295, April 30, 1802. Cf. also *Br.* II, 23, and *Br.* I, 208.

13. He was to refer, but not defer, to Wolf in his Academy addresses on hermeneutics and criticism (1829–1830).

14. None of this correspondence has been preserved.

15. *Br.* I, 319, Aug. 19, 1802.

16. *Br.* I, 207, Mar. 23, 1799.

17. *Soliloquies*, 74.

18. *On What Gives Value to Life*, 32-33.

19. *Soliloquies*, 28-31. I have altered Friess's translation somewhat. Schleiermacher's 1792 New Year's sermon also rings with this theme. See *Fifteen Sermons* (trans. Lawler, 2003), 13-30. The volume includes other New Year's sermons from 1791, 1793, 1794, and 1797.

20. *Soliloquies*, 30-31. Italics added. I have revised some parts of Friess's translation here.

21. See Maynard Solomon, *Late Beethoven: Music, Thought, Imagination* (Berkeley: University of California Press, 2003), 101.

22. For the following data cf. Wolfgang Ribbe, ed., *Geschichte Berlins: Von der Frühgeschichte bis zur Industrialisierung* (vol. 1; Munich: C. H. Beck, 1985), 413-19.

23. I have told the Anglo-American story in *The Cambridge Companion to Friedrich Schleiermacher* (ed. Jacqueline Mariña; Cambridge Companions to Religion; Cambridge: Cambridge University Press, 2005).

2. Schleiermacher's Perspective on Religious Experience

1. Naturally, this is only a highly plausible reconstruction but one based on a rather intimate knowledge of Schleiermacher's life. *Experience (Erfahrung)* was a term Schleiermacher himself infrequently used in this connection, though the term's accrued meanings since his lifetime make it seem appropriate today.

2. See my 2003 essay on this subject.

3. A Systematic Summary of Schleiermacher's Theology

1. It is no accident that those propositions begin with a treatment of election and end with an appendix examining the rejected doctrine of "eternal damnation." Universal salvation is taken to be the will and act of God from the foundation of the earth.

2. Note that in §83.1 conscience in relation to what is good and as an accompaniment of one's consciousness of the need for redemption can be conceived as such a divine revelation in inner experience.

3. This *Introduction* has been issued in a rough English translation by John Shelley (1989) that understandably does not try to follow principles for a critical edition.

4. Hermann Peiter will issue a painstakingly comparative presentation from almost word-perfect student transcripts. I expect that an English translation will follow in due course. As an indispensable complement, I am seeing to an even earlier collection of Peiter's numerous essays on the subject over the years (he is in retirement) including three English translations of recent essays.

5. I draw this account especially from one of his essays on Schleiermacher's Christian ethics: "The Autonomy of Theological Ethics . . . A Schleiermacher Interpretation," initially issued in *Papers of the Schleiermacher Group and Schleiermacher Society* (ed. David E. Klemm and Terrence N. Tice; American Academy of Religion Annual Meeting; San Francisco, 1997). This essay is also to appear in the collection of Peiter's essays on Schleiermacher's Christian Ethics and Reviews on Schleiermacher Studies mentioned in the previous note.

4. Definitions from Schleiermacher's Discourse

1. See his sermonic treatise on *The Christian Household* (1818), where he enjoins parents, heads of households, leaders and managers of public affairs, and other enterprises to exercise such care among those in their charge. See also his sermons on proclamation* by word and deed in the steps of Jesus.

2. John Dewey, *Individualism Old and New* (New York: Minton, Balch & Co., 1930), 171; still in print.

3. Eph. 4:15 (see Tice, "Speaking the Truth in Love," 2002).

4. John Hick, *Evil and the God of Love* (New York: Harper & Row, 1966), 403; 2nd ed. (London: Macmillan, 1977), 389.

5. On not adding *the* before *Christian Faith*, or before *Christian Ethics* for that matter, see Wilfred Cantwell Smith, "On Mistranslated Book Titles," *Religious Studies* 20, no. 1 (March 1984): 27-42, especially 34-42.

6. Philosopher Mortimer Adler's *How to Read a Book: The Art of Getting a Liberal Education* (New York: Simon and Schuster, 1940), ix, 398. This highly valuable work, by the eventual founder of the Great Books program, has been in print since 1940. A revised and updated edition, by Adler and Charles van Doren, was issued by the same publisher in 1972 (see xiv, 426).

7. The adjective *fromm* is often more suitably translated "religious," to obviate making such misidentifications.

8. Rom. 8:21. Even the obedience of the regenerate is "free" (CF §112.1).

SELECTED BIBLIOGRAPHY

These works are almost all in English, all but a few of them published since 1960, when I began gathering the Schleiermacher literature in all languages. Some key resources in German are listed in the first three sections. These contain further helpful bibliographies, as does *The Cambridge Companion to Friedrich Schleiermacher* (ed. Jacqueline Mariña; Cambridge Companions to Religion; Cambridge: Cambridge University Press, 2005). Only a few articles can be included.

Bibliographies

Arndt, Andreas, and Wolfgang Virmond. *Schleiermachers Briefwechsel (Verzeichnis) vebst einer Liste seiner Vorlesungen*. Volume 11 of *Schleiermacher-Archiv*. Berlin/New York: Walter de Gruyter, 1992. Page 330.

Meding, Wichmann von. *Bibliographie der Schriften Schleiermachers nebst einer Zusammenstellung und Datierung seiner gedruckten Predigten*. Berlin/New York: Walter de Gruyter, 1992. Page 367.

Nowak, Kurt. *Schleiermacher*. Göttingen: Vandenhoeck & Ruprecht, 2001. Page 632. [See the selected bibliography, 579-600.]

Tice, Terrence N. *Schleiermacher Bibliography*. 2 vols. Princeton: Princeton University Press, 1966, 1985. Pages 119, 168. [Updates: Listing of additions and corrections in the 1985 bibliography are also contained as part of succeeding updates in *New Athenaeum/Neues Athenaeum* 1 (1989), 2 (1991), and 4 (1995); a final update is forthcoming.]

————. *Schleiermacher's Sermons: A Chronological Listing and Account*. Lewiston, N.Y.: Edwin Mellen Press, 1997. Page 181.

Collected Works

Schleiermacher, Friedrich. *Friedrich Schleiermachers Sämmtliche Werke*. 31 vols. Berlin: Reimer, 1834–1864. [The collection is divided into three parts: I. Theologie (11 vols.); II. Predigten (10 vols.); Philosophie (10 vols.).]

————. *Kritische Gesamtausgabe*. Berlin/New York: Walter de Gruyter, 1984–. [To appear in five parts: I. *Schriften und Entwürfe*; II. *Vorlesungen*; III. *Predigten*; IV. *Übersetzungen*; V. *Briefwechsel*. Many volumes have appeared; none contain his preaching or translations.]

————. *Schleiermachers Werke: Auswahl*. Vols. 1-2. Edited by Otto Braun and Johannes Bauer. 2nd ed. Aalen: Scientia Verlag, 1981. [1st ed. 1910, 1913; 2nd ed., 1928, 1927 respectively. This material contains his philosophical ethics. Volumes 3 and 4 contain other writings, reprinted in 1821. All these volumes are useful for their introductions and indexes.]

Biography

Kantzenbach, Friedrich Wilhelm. *Schleiermacher*. Reinbek bei Hamburg: Rowohlt-Taschenbuch-Verlag, 1967. Page 179. [Full of pictures.]

Nowak, Kurt. *Schleiermacher*. Göttingen: Vandenhoeck & Ruprecht, 2001. Page 632.

Redeker, Martin. *Schleiermacher: Life and Thought*. Translated by John Wallhausser. Philadelphia: Fortress Press, 1973. Page 221.

Willich, Ehrenfried von. *Aus Schleiermachers Hause: Jugenderrinerungen seines Stiefsonnes*. Berlin: Reimer, 1909. Pages iv, 220.

Schleiermacher's Works in English Translation

Translations have been appearing fairly regularly over the past twenty-five years and are still coming. More translators are needed. This listing is alphabetical by title.

"The Boat Ride." Translated by Michael D. Ryan. *New Athenaeum/Neues Athenaeum* 2 (1991): 171-74.

Brief Outline of Theology as a Field of Study. Translated by Terrence N. Tice. Lewiston, N.Y.: Edwin Mellen Press, 1990. Pages xii, 230. [This volume contains the 1811 and 1830 editions; originally on the 1830 edition alone. Atlanta: John Knox Press, 1966.]

Brouillon zur Ethik: Notes on Ethics (1804–1806). Translated and edited by John Wallhausser and Terrence N. Tice with consultation from Edwina Lawler. Lewiston, N.Y.: Edwin Mellen Press, 2002. Pages xiii, 289.

Christian Caring: Selections from Practical Theology. Edited by James O. Duke and Howard W. Stone. Translated by James O. Duke. Philadelphia: Fortress Press, 1988. Page 127.

The Christian Faith. Translated by H. R. MacKintosh, J. S. Stewart, et al. from the 2nd ed. of 1830–1831. Edinburgh: T&T Clark, 1928. Pages xii, 760. [Original German of first edition (1821–1822): *Der christliche Glaube nach den Grundsätzen der evangelischen Kirche in Zusammenhange dargestellt*. 3 vols. Edited by Hermann Peiter, KGA I/7.1-3. Berlin/New York: Walter de Gruyter, 1980, 1983. The 697-page vol. 3 contains invaluable marginal notes and an appendix, including quotations of material cited by Schleiermacher. Original German of the 2nd ed. (1830–1831): *Der christliche Glaube nach den Grundsätzen der evangelischen Kirche im Zusammenhange dargestellt*. Berlin: Georg Reimer. The 7th ed. of this 1830–1831 work is in 2 vols. Edited by Martin Redeker. Berlin/New York: Walter de Gruyter, 1960; Repr. in 1999 and still useful, despite a few errors. The KGA I/11, edited by Rolf Schäfer, is chiefly a record of the original copyediting and has no index.]

Christian Faith (1830–1831). Translated by Terrence N. Tice, Catherine L. Kelsey, and Edwina Lawler. Louisville: Westminster John Knox Press, 2005.

The Christian Household: A Sermonic Treatise (1820). Translated by Dietrich Seidel and Terrence N. Tice. Lewiston, N.Y.: Edwin Mellen Press, 1991. Pages xli, 237.

Christmas Eve (1827). Translated by Terrence N. Tice. Richmond: John Knox Press, 1967. Repr., Lewiston, N.Y.: Edwin Mellen Press, 1991. Page 92. [Forthcoming: a new revised translation by Terrence N. Tice of the 1806 and 1827 editions.]

"Comparison of the Political Philosophies of Plato and Aristotle" (1794). Translated by Esther D. Reed and Kostas Neafas. *New Athenaeum/Neues Athenaeum* 6 (2001): 33-50.

Dialectic, or the Art of Doing Philosophy: A Study Edition of the 1811 Notes. Translated by Terrence N. Tice. American Academy of Religion: Texts and Translations Series 11. Edited by Terry Godlove. Atlanta: Scholars Press, 1996. Repr., Oxford: Oxford University Press, 2004. Pages xxv, 92.

Fifteen Sermons of Friedrich Schleiermacher Delivered to Celebrate the Beginning of a New Year. Translated and edited by Edwina Lawler. Lewiston, N.Y.: Edwin Mellen Press, 2003. Pages lxxxiii, 282.

Hermeneutics: The Handwritten Manuscripts. Edited by Heinz Kimmerle. Translated by Jack Forstman and James O. Duke. Missoula, Mont.: Scholars Press, 1977. Pages v, 252.

Hermeneutics and Criticism. Translated by Terrence N. Tice. [In preparation in a different configuration and including all the exegetical material.]

Hermeneutics and Criticism and Other Writings. Translated by Andrew W. Bowie. Cambridge: Cambridge University Press, 1998. Pages xl, 284.

Hermeneutics, Criticism and Translation: Academy Addresses 1815, 1829–1830. Edited and translated by Terrence N. Tice. In preparation.

"Idea for a Rational Catechism for Noble Women" (1798). Translated by Robert F. Streetman. *New Athenaeum/Neues Athenaeum* 2 (1991): 175-76.

Introduction to Christian Ethics. Translated by John C. Shelley. Nashville: Abingdon, 1989. Page 108. [1831 "Introduction"—the remaining lectures were yet to be published.]

Lectures on Philosophical Ethics (1812–1814). Edited by Robert B. Loudon. Translated by Louise Adey Huish. Cambridge: Cambridge University Press, 2002. Pages xl, 253.

Letters on the Occasion of the Political Theological Task and the Sendschreiben (Open Letter of Jewish Heads of Households) (1800). Translated by Gilya Gerda Schmidt. Lewiston, N.Y.: Edwin Mellen Press, 2001. Page 90. See also *A Debate on Jewish Emancipation and Christian Theology in Old Berlin/ David Friedlander, Friedrich Schleiermacher, Wilhelm Abraham Teller.* Edited and translated by Richard Crouter and Julie Klassen. Indianapolis: Hackett, 2004. Pages xiii, 177. See also Crouter's article in the Monographs section.

The Life of Jesus. Edited by Jack C. Verheyden. Translated by Maclean Gilmore. Philadelphia: Fortress Press, 1975. Pages lxii, 481. Repr., Mifflintown: Sigler, 1997.

Luke: A Critical Study (1817). Edited by Terrence N. Tice. Translated by Connop Thirlwall. Lewiston, N.Y.: Edwin Mellen Press, 1993. Pages vi, 372.

"Notes on Aristotle: *Nichomachean Ethics* 8-9." Translated by Michael Welker. *Theology Today* 56 (1999): 164-68.

Occasional Thoughts on Universities in the German Sense with an Appendix Regarding a University Soon to be Established (1808). Translated by Terrence N. Tice with Edwina Lawler. Lewiston, N.Y.: Edwin Mellen Press, 1991, 2005. Pages iv, 92. [Also in *Writings on Academia.* Lewiston, N.Y.: Edwin Mellen Press, forthcoming.]

"On Colossians 1:15-20" (1832). Translated by Esther D. Reed and Alan Braley. *New Athenaeum/Neues Athenaeum* 5 (1998): 48-80.

On Creeds, Confessions and Church Union: "That They May Be One." Edited and translated by Iain G. Nicol. Lewiston, N.Y.: Edwin Mellen Press, 2004. Pages ii, 265.

On Election (1819). Translated by Iain G. Nicol and Allen Jorgensen. In preparation.

On Freedom (1792–1793). Translated by Albert L. Blackwell. Lewiston, N.Y.: Edwin Mellen Press, 1992. Pages xlvi, 155.

On Religion: Addresses in Response to Its Cultured Critics. 1821 edition. Translated by Terrence N. Tice. Richmond: John Knox Press, 1969. Page 383. [A new revised translation of the 1799, 1806, and 1821 editions is in preparation by Terrence N. Tice.]

On Religion: Speeches to Its Cultured Despisers. 1799 edition. Translated by Richard Crouter. Cambridge: Cambridge University Press, 1988; 2nd ed., 1996. Pages xlv, 128.

On Religion: Speeches to Its Cultured Despisers (1821). Translated by John Oman. Louisville: Westminster John Knox Press, 1994. Pages xiv, 287. [Original edition from London: Routledge & Kegan Paul, 1894; then New York: Harper, 1958.]

"On the Discrepancy between the Sabellian and Athanasian Method of Representing the Doctrine of the Trinity" (1822). Translated by Moses Stuart. *Biblical Repository and Quarterly Observer* 5 (April 1835): 31-53, and 6 (July 1835): 1-116. [A new translation is forthcoming in Terrence N. Tice, *The Triune God.* Lewiston, N.Y.: Edwin Mellen Press.]

On the Glaubenslehre: Two Letters to Dr. Lücke (1829). Translated by James O. Duke and Francis Fiorenza. Chico, Calif.: Scholars Press, 1981. Pages ix, 136. [A revised edition is in preparation.]

On the Highest Good (1789). Translated by H. Victor Froese. Lewiston, N.Y.: Edwin Mellen Press, 1992. Pages iv, 149.

"On the Worth of Socrates as a Philosopher" (1815). Translated by Connop Thirlwall. In *Life of Socrates.* Edited by Gustav Friedrich Wiggers. London, 1840. Page 85.

On What Gives Value to Life (1793–1794). Translated by Edwina Lawler and Terrence N. Tice. Lewiston, N.Y.: Edwin Mellen Press, 1995. Pages xxxii, 112.

Psychology. Translated by Edwina Lawler. Lewiston, N.Y.: Edwin Mellen Press, in preparation.

Reformed but Ever Reforming: Sermons in Relation to the Celebration of the Handing over of the Augsburg Confession (1830). Translated and edited by Iain G. Nicol. Lewiston, N.Y.: Edwin Mellen Press, 1997. Pages xxviii, 185.

"Schleiermacher's Note on the Knowledge of Freedom" (1790–1792), "Schleiermacher's Notes on Kant's *Critique of Practical Reason*" (probably from 1790), and "Schleiermacher's Review of Immanuel Kant's *Anthropology from a Pragmatic Point of View*" (1799). Translated by Jacqueline Mariña. *New Athenaeum/Neues Athenaeum* 5 (1998): 11-31.

Selected Sermons of Schleiermacher. Translated by Mary F. Wilson. London: Hodder and Stoughton, 1890. Pages viii, 451.

Servant of the Word: Selected Sermons of Schleiermacher. Translated by Dawn DeVries. Philadelphia: Fortress Press, 1987. Pages x, 230.

Soliloquies: An English Translation of the Monologen. Translated by Horace Leland Friess. Chicago: Open Court, 1926. Pages xl, 176. See also parts 2 and 3 of *The Early Political Writings of the German Romantics.* Edited and translated by Frederick C. Beiser. Cambridge: Cambridge University Press, 1996. [A new translation, by Tice, of all its editions is in preparation.]

"To Cecilie" (1789–1790). Translated by Edwina Lawler. *New Athenaeum/Neues Athenaeum* 6 (2001): 11-34.

"Toward a Theory of Sociable Conduct." Translated by Jeffery Hoover. *New Athenaeum/Neues Athenaeum* 4 (1995): 20-39.

Major Collections

In the following major collections (fourteen from Edwin Mellen Press) some essays are in languages other than English due to their international character. In contrast, very few English essays appear in the several German collections, the largest of which heads the list here. *New Athenaeum/Neues Athenaeum*, thus far in seven volumes, also includes collections of essays, some of them in German; volume 6 is dedicated to Wolfgang Virmond; volume 7 is a Festschrift for Hermann Patsch (2005).

Barth, Ülrich, and Claus-Dieter Ostövener, eds., *200 Jahre "Reden über die Religion": Akten des 1. Internationalen Kongress der Schleiermacher-Gesellschaft, Halle 14.17 März, 1999.* Volume 19 of *Schleiermacher-Archiv.* Berlin/New York: Walter de Gruyter, 2000. Pages xiii, 987.

Dierkes, Hans, Ruth Richardson Ragovin, and Terrence N. Tice, eds. *Schleiermacher, Romanticism and the Critical Arts: A Festschrift in Honor of Hermann Patsch. New Athenaeum/Neues Athenaeum* 7. Lewiston, N.Y.: Edwin Mellen Press, 2005.

Duke, James O., and Robert F. Streetman, eds. *Barth and Schleiermacher: Beyond the Impasse?* Philadelphia: Fortress Press, 1988. Pages xiii, 186.

Funk, Robert W., ed. *Schleiermacher as Contemporary.* New York: Herder & Herder, 1970. Page 215.

Mariña, Jacqueline, ed. *The Cambridge Companion to Schleiermacher.* Cambridge: Cambridge University Press, 2005.

Nicol, Iain G., ed. *Schleiermacher and Feminism: Sources, Evaluations and Responses.* Lewiston, N.Y.: Edwin Mellen Press, 1992. Pages iv, 127.

Richardson, Ruth Drucilla, ed. *New Athenaeum/Neues Athenaeum.* Lewiston, N.Y.: Edwin Mellen Press, 1989–.[Through 2005, seven volumes of collected essays and resources have appeared.]

———. *Schleiermacher in Context: Papers from the 1988 International Symposium on Schleiermacher at Herrnhut, the German Democratic Republic.* Lewiston, N.Y.: Edwin Mellen Press, 1991. Page 459.

Richardson, Ruth Drucilla, and Edwina Lawler, eds. *Understanding Schleiermacher: From Translation to Interpretation; A Festschrift in Honor of Terrence Nelson Tice*. Lewiston, N.Y.: Edwin Mellen Press, 1998. Pages xvi, 624. [The volume includes a bibliography of Tice's writings.]

Monographs, Mostly in English

For other listings of Schleiermacher studies see *On Religion: Speeches to Its Cultured Despisers*. 1799 ed. Translated by Richard Crouter. Cambridge: Cambridge University Press, 1988; 2nd ed., 1996; *Hermeneutics and Criticism and Other Writings*. Translated by Andrew W. Bowie. Cambridge: Cambridge University Press, 1998; and *The Cambridge Companion to Friedrich Schleiermacher* (ed. Jacqueline Mariña; Cambridge Companions to Religion; Cambridge: Cambridge University Press, 2005). [Also see other editions of Schleiermacher's works listed above.]

Barth, Karl. *Protestant Thought in the Nineteenth Century*. New York: Simon and Schuster, 1969. Page 435.

————. *The Theology of Schleiermacher: Lectures in Göttingen, Winter Semester of 1923–24*. Edited by Dietrich Ritschl. Grand Rapids, Mich.: Eerdmans, 1982. Pages xix, 287.

Berner, Christian. *La Philosophie de Schleiermacher*. Paris: Cerf, 1995. Page 281. [Outstanding; the only work in French listed here.]

Birkner, Hans-Joachim. *Schleiermacher-Studien*. Edited by Hermann Fischer. Volume 16 of *Schleiermacher-Archiv*. Berlin/New York: Walter de Gruyter, 1996. Pages xvi, 421. [The volume includes a bibliography of Birkner's writings, by Aushulf von Scheliha.]

Blackwell, Albert L. "The Role of Music in Schleiermacher's Writings." Pages 439-48 in *Internationaler Schleiermacher Kongress Berlin 1984*. Edited by Kurt-Victor Selge. Berlin/New York: Walter de Gruyter, 1985.

————. "Schleiermacher on Musical Experience and Religious Experience." Pages 121-49 in *Friedrich Schleiermacher and the Founding of the University of Berlin: The Study of Religion as a Scientific Discipline*. Edited by Herbert Richardson. Lewiston, N.Y.: Edwin Mellen Press, 1991.

————. *Schleiermacher's Early Philosophy of Life: Determinism, Freedom, and Phantasy*. Chico, Calif.: Scholars Press, 1982. Pages xii, 327.

Boekels, Joachim. *Schleiermacher als Kirchengeschichtler, mit Edition der Nachschrift Karl Rudolf Hagenbachs von 1821/22*. Volume 13 of *Schleiermacher-Archiv*. Berlin/New York: Walter de Gruyter, 1994. Pages xi, 488.

Bowie, Andrew. "Schleiermacher, Habermas and Rorty." Pages 216-32 in *Schleiermachers Dialektik: Liebe zum Wissen in Philosophie und Theologie*. Edited by Christine Helmer, Christianne Krannich, and Brigit Rehme-Iffert. Tübingen: Mohr Siebeck, 2003.

Boyd, George N. "Schleiermacher's 'Über den Unterschied Zwischen Naturgesetz und Sittengesetz.'" *Journal of Religious Ethics* 17 (1989): 41-50.

Brandt, James M. *All Things New: Reform of Church and Society in Schleiermacher's Christian Ethics*. Louisville: Westminster John Knox Press, 2001. Pages xvii, 160.

Brandt, Richard B. *The Philosophy of Schleiermacher: The Development of His Theory of Scientific and Religious Knowledge*. New York, 1941. Repr., New York: Greenwood, 1968. Pages viii, 350.

Capetz, Paul F. *Christian Faith as Religion: A Study in the Theologies of Calvin and Schleiermacher*. Lanham: University Press of America, 1998. Page 313.

Clements, Keith W., ed. *Friedrich Schleiermacher: Pioneer of Modern Theology*. San Francisco: Collins, 1987. Page 281.

Crossley, John P., Jr. "The Ethical Impulse in Schleiermacher's Early Ethics." *Journal of Religious Ethics* 17 (1989): 5-24. [See also John Crossley, "Schleiermacher's Christian Ethics in

Relation to His Philosophical Ethics," in *Annual of the Society of Christian Ethics* 18 (1998): 93-117.]

Crouter, Richard. "Schleiermacher's Letters on the Occasion and the Crisis of Berlin Jewry." Pages 74-91 in *Ethical Monotheism, Past and Present: Essays in Honor of Wendell S. Dietrich*. Edited by Theodore M. Vial and Mark Hadley. *Brown Judaic Studies* 329. Providence, R.I.: Brown Judaic Studies, 2001.

Curran, Thomas H. *Doctrine and Speculation in Schleiermacher's Glaubenslehre*. Berlin/New York: Walter de Gruyter, 1994. Pages xx, 390.

DeVries, Dawn. *Jesus Christ in the Preaching of Calvin and Schleiermacher*. Louisville: Westminster John Knox Press, 1996. Pages x, 115.

Frank, Manfred. *Das individualle Allgemeine: Textstrukurierung und interpretation nach Schleiermacher*. Frankfurt am Main: Suhrkamp, 1977; 2nd printing, 1985. Page 382.

Gerrish, Brian A. *Continuing the Reformation: Essays on Modern Religious Thought*. Chicago: University of Chicago Press, 1993. Pages xv, 283.

———. *A Prince of the Church: Schleiermacher and the Beginnings of Modern Theology*. Philadelphia: Fortress Press, 1984. Page 79.

Guenther-Gleason, Patricia Ellen. *On Schleiermacher and Gender Politics*. Harrisburg, Pa.: Trinity Press International, 1997. Pages xxiv, 353.

Helmer, Christine, et al., eds. *Schleiermacher and Whitehead: Open Systems in Dialogue*. Berlin/New York: Walter de Gruyter, 2004. Pages xii, 356.

Herms, Eilert. *Menschsein im Werden: Studien zu Schleiermacher*. Tübingen: Mohr Siebeck, 2003. Pages viii, 502.

Hick, John. *Evil and the God of Love*. Rev. ed. New York: Harper & Row, 1978. Pages x, 389.

Kelsey, Catherine L. *Thinking about Christ with Schleiermacher*. Louisville: Westminster John Knox Press, 2003. Pages viii, 126.

Lamm, Julia A. *The Living God: Schleiermacher's Theological Appropriation of Spinoza*. University Park, Pa.: Pennsylvania State University Press, 1996. Pages x, 246.

Lawler, Edwina. "Neohumanistic and Idealistic Conceptions of a University." Pages 1-44 in *Friedrich Schleiermacher and the Founding of the University of Berlin*. Edited by Herbert Richardson. Lewiston, N.Y.: Edwin Mellen Press, 1991.

Mariña, Jacqueline. "Schleiermacher's Christology Revisited: A Reply to His Critics." *Scottish Journal of Theology* 49, no. 2 (1996): 177-200.

———. "Schleiermacher on the Outpourings of the Inner Fire: Experiential Expressivism and Religious Pluralism." *Religious Studies* 40 (2004): 125-43.

Niebuhr, Richard R. "Schleiermacher and the Names of God: A Consideration of Schleiermacher in Relation to Our Theism." Pages 176-205 in *Schleiermacher as Contemporary*. Edited by Robert W. Funk. New York: Herder & Herder, 1970.

———. *Schleiermacher on Christ and Religion: A New Introduction*. New York: Charles Scribner's Sons, 1964.

Nowak, Kurt. "Schleiermacher als Prediger am Charité-Krankenhaus in Berlin (1796–1802)." *Theologische Zeitschrift* 41 (1985): 391-411.

Park, John Sungmin. *Theological Ethics of Friedrich Schleiermacher*. Lewiston, N.Y.: Edwin Mellen Press, 2001. Page 163.

Patsch, Hermann. *Alle Menschen sind Kunstler: Friedrich Schleiermachers poetische Versuche*. Volume 2 of *Schleiermacher-Archiv*. Berlin/New York: Walter de Gruyter, 1986. Pages x, 254.

Pickle, Joseph W. "How Comparative Religion Could Have Been Studied in Schleiermacher's University of Berlin." Pages 83-120 in *Schleiermacher and the Founding of the University of Berlin*. Edited by Herbert Richardson. Lewiston, N.Y.: Edwin Mellen Press, 1991.

Redeker, Martin. *Schleiermacher: Life and Thought.* Translated by John Wallhausser. Philadelphia: Fortress Press, 1973. Page 221.

Reich, Andreas. *Friedrich Schleiermacher als Pfarrer an der Dreifaltigkeitskirche 1809–1834.* Volume 12 of *Schleiermacher-Archiv.* Berlin/New York: Walter de Gruyter, 1992. Pages xii, 568.

Scholtz, Gunter. *Schleiermachers Musikphilosophie.* Göttingen: Vandenhoeck & Ruprecht, 1981. Page 171.

Schurr, Johannes. *Schleiermachers Theorie der Erziehung: Interpretationen zur Pädagogikvorlesung von 1826.* Düsseldorf: Schwann, 1975. Page 560.

Sockness, Brent W. "Was Schleiermacher a Virtue Ethicist? *Tugend* and *Bildung* in the Early Writings," *Zeitschrift für neuere Theologiegeschichte* 8 (2001): 1-33.

Sonderegger, Katherine. "Theological Realism." Pages 195-215 in *Ethical Monotheism, Past and Present: Essays in Honor of Wendell S. Dietrich.* Edited by Theodore M. Vial and Mark Hadley. *Brown Judaic Studies* 329. Providence, R.I.: Brown Judaic Studies, 2001. [On Schleiermacher's account of the subject.]

Stein, Craig. *Schleiermacher's Construction of the Subject in the Introduction to Christian Faith in Light of M. Foucault's Critique of Modern Knowledge.* Lewiston, N.Y.: Edwin Mellen Press, 2001. Pages x, 201.

Thandeka. *The Embodied Self: Friedrich Schleiermacher's Solution to Kant's Problem of the Empirical Self.* Albany: State University of New York Press, 1995. Pages xiv, 151.

Thiel, John E. *Imagination and Authority: Theological Authorship in the Modern Tradition.* Minneapolis: Fortress Press, 1991. Pages xii, 228.

Tice, Terrence N. "Enlightenment, Romantic and Modern Elements in Schleiermacher's Thought." In *Schleiermacher, Romanticism and the Critical Arts: A Festschrift in Honor of Hermann Patsch.* Edited by Hans Dierkes, Ruth Ragovin, and Terrence N. Tice. *New Athenaeum/Neues Athenaeum* 7. Lewiston, N.Y.: Edwin Mellen Press, 2005.

————. "Indications of What Schleiermacher's Thought Is Good for Today." Pages 605-15 in *Understanding Schleiermacher: From Translation to Interpretation; A Festschrift in Honor of Terrence Nelson Tice.* Edited by Ruth Drucilla Richardson and Edwina Lawler. Lewiston, N.Y.: Edwin Mellen Press, 1998.

————. "Schleiermacher on the Scientific Study of Religion." Pages 45-82 in *Schleiermacher and the Founding of the University of Berlin.* Edited by Herbert Richardson. Lewiston, N.Y.: Edwin Mellen Press, 1991.

————. "Schleiermacher Yesterday, Today and Tomorrow." In *Cambridge Companion to Friedrich Schleiermacher.* Edited by Jacqueline Mariña. Cambridge: Cambridge University Press, 2005.

————. "Schleiermacher's Conception of Ministry: Proclamation in the Christian Life." In *Festschrift in Honor of Michael Ryan.* Lewiston, N.Y.: Edwin Mellen Press, forthcoming.

————. "Schleiermacher's Conception of Religion." Pages 332-56 in *Schleiermacher.* Edited by Marco M. Olivetti. *Archivio di Filosofia.* Rome, 1984.

————. "Schleiermacher's Psychology: An Early Modern Approach, a Challenge to Current Tendencies." Pages 509-21 in *Schleiermacher und die wissenschaftliche Kultur des Christentums.* Edited by Gunter Meckenstock and Joachim Ringleben. Berlin/New York: Walter de Gruyter, 1991.

————. "Schleiermacher's Theological Method." 3 vols. PhD diss., Princeton Theological Seminary, 1961. [Available from University Microfilms.]

————. "Schleiermacher's Theology: Ecclesial and Scientific, Ecumenical and Reformed." Pages 386-407 in *Probing the Reformed Tradition: Historical Studies in Honor of Edward A. Dowey, Jr.* Louisville: Westminster John Knox Press, 1989.

————. "Schleiermacher's Use of Philosophical Mindedness in Theology." Pages 78-88 in *Schleiermachers Dialektik: Die Liebe zum Wissen in Philosophie und Theologie.* Edited by

Christine Helmer, Christiane Krannich, and Birgit Rehme-Iffert. Tübingen: Mohr Siebeck, 2003.

———. "Speaking the Truth in Love: Schleiermacher's Perspectives on Church Government and Service." *Toronto Journal of Theology* 18, no. 1 (2002): 21-32. [Festschrift for Iain G. Nicol.]

———. "Translation as a Philosophical Art." *New Athenaeum/Neues Athenaeum* 5 (1998): 115-28.

———. *Schleiermacher's Sermons: A Chronological Listing and Account.* Lewiston, N.Y.: Edwin Mellen Press, 1997. Page 181.

Töpelmann, Roger. *Romantische Freundschaft und Frömmigkeit: Briefe des Berliner Verlagers Georg Andreas Reimer an Friedrich Daniel Ernst Schleiermacher.* Spolia Berolinensia 16. Hildesheim: Weidmann, 1999. Page 372.

Vance, Robert Lee. *Sin and Self-Consciousness in the Thought of Friedrich Schleiermacher.* Lewiston, N.Y.: Edwin Mellen Press, 1994. Page 219.

Wallhausser, John. "Schleiermacher's Critique of Ethical Reason: Toward a Systematic Ethics." *Journal of Religious Ethics* 17 (1989): 25-39.

Welker, Michael. "'We Live Deeper than We Think': The Genius of Schleiermacher's Earliest Ethics," *Theology Today* 56 (1999): 169-79.

Williams, Robert R. *Schleiermacher the Theologian: The Construction of the Doctrine of God.* Philadelphia: Fortress Press, 1978. Pages xiii, 196.

Wyman, Walter E., Jr. "Testing Liberalism's Conceptuality: The Relation of Sin and Evil in Schleiermacher's Theology." Pages 138-54 in *Ethical Monotheism, Past and Present: Essays in Honor of Wendell S. Dietrich.* Edited by Theodore M. Vial and Mark Hadley. *Brown Judaic Studies* 329. Providence, R.I.: Brown Judaic Studies, 2001.

INDEX OF NAMES AND PLACES

These indexes are designed to help capture the content and texture of Schleiermacher's life and thought. They are also conceived as tools to augment further exploration. Although "definition" pages are marked in bold print, they do not, of course, present the only defining features. With occasional exceptions, where full names and dates are not given in the chapters they are included here.

INDEX OF SUBJECTS, WRITINGS, AND CONCEPTS